Rise Up

How Great Leaders Stand Out and Get Promoted

By Becky A. Thomas

Be Greater Press

For a Spotify playlist that contains corresponding songs to the title of each chapter please visit www.begreaterconsulting.com/book password: rockon. All first names mentioned in this book are fictional for educational purposes and do not represent real people.

Published in the United States by Be Greater Press.
www.begreaterpress.com

Be Greater Press

ISBN 978-0-578-44776-6

Editor: Ross J. Kelly
Cover design: Daniel O. Ojedokun
Author Photograph: Will Byington

First Edition: January 2019

10 9 8 7 6 5 4 3 2 1

DEDICATION

Thank you to my parents Joe & Lynne
and my favorite sister Carrie
for your love and support throughout this journey.

BOOK REVIEW PARTY CREW!

Special Thanks to my Book Review Party Crew for all your help in reviewing content along the way! I'm so lucky to have such a great group of supportive friends!

ACKNOWLEDGEMENTS

Big shout out to my editor extraordinaire, Ross Kelly. You were able to "herd the cats in my mind" and make sense of it all. Thank you for your patience, support, laughter and insights. You have the patience of a saint, and I am so glad we were able to work together. It's been a fun ride! Additional thanks to my proofreaders Quinn and Christine for last minute reviews and to my two contributors whose work includes 65 Back by Ram Ramanathan, and The Knock Method: 8 Steps to Building Thriving Career Relationships by Rebecca Leder. Thank you both for contributing your work.

A special thank you to Lisa McHugh (because you are still Lisa McHugh to me) for believing in me no matter what crazy idea I have. Your response, "If anyone can do it, you can!" has been the one thing I hang on to on during those tougher days of the entrepreneurial adventure.

The student has become the teacher in Marla, who always reminded me "If you can believe it, you can achieve it!" And that reminder is a welcome one. Thank you. And to Deb and Sarah for our outings throughout the year that were much needed breaks from the madness. Thank you for all your support. Speaking of breaks, thank you to Tiffany for creating some awesome music promo videos with me and being my hype man. I always love laughing with you!

The "Spin Six". (Allison, Carrie, Christy, Colleen, Michelle, Peters and Metzger), you are the definition of loyalty. Your love and support has been amazing and may our Martini Madnesses continue until we can't hear each other anymore. It's already started happening anyway. Ahah...

My Iowa crew. Shan, Kross, Rach, Heather, Colleen. First, Go Hawks! And second, I love our memories like lost shoes after parties and chippin' out. The laughs continue with new stories, and I am thinking we need to make the Cubs weekend a tradition!! DG ladies, thanks as always for your loyalty and support, ITB.

The dinner crew!! A welcome relief with Buzz, Debbie, Sarah, Sean, Trudy, Vanessa, Will, and sometimes Vic with a side of Lionel. Thanks for keeping me nourished.

My Italian friends. Grazie mille come sempre, TVB!!! Amy, thank you for always being my little angel and coaching buddy. Audra, your support throughout this journey has been amazing, thank you. Kasia & Jeff, I'm putting you in this group too. Thank you so much for your expertise and loyal support throughout this process. Libby and Mandy, you're practically Italian at this point anyway. Love our travels and adventures, thanks for all your support this year.

A special note to the coaching community. Thank you to the Coaches Training Institute (CTI) and Susan Valdiserri for being an inspiration throughout my whole coaching journey, and Kathy Ball-Toncic for being an amazing coach. Thanks to the Leadership Circle for your amazing assessment tool and Mike for all your continued support. Unfortunately, I never got to meet Dr. Susan Jeffers, but want to thank her for her book, which inspired me to look further into coaching. Judith E. Glaser was one special coach that had me learning non-stop. She left us too soon, but I will take her support and kind words with me always. I'd also like to thank Marshall Goldsmith for being the coolest coach out there! Thank you for your kind words and for sparking the idea for me to write this book!

Table of Contents

Introduction

Start Me Up

A few years back, I went on a trip to South Africa with my family for my mom's birthday. While my sister Carrie went for a swim with the sharks, my parents and I had a tour guide take us around to see different parts of Cape Town. Our driver shared with us that he was from England but had lived in South Africa for the past 30 years.

"We're from Chicago," I told him. "But I am currently living in Rome, Italy."

"Oh those Eyyetalians!" he said. "They're like peacocks, they are. Struttin' their stuff around all the time, like 'Look at me with all my good looks and fashion!' I've never seen anything like it!"

Ahhh, the peacock . . . nature's ultimate icon of "Look at me!" These colorful creatures use their oversized and impressively patterned plumage to create the perception of being larger than they are so they can intimidate potential predators, and to serve as an attention-grabbing courtship ritual to attract a mate.

Are we any different? The answer is no, we are not!

Although my Italian friends are not quite to the extreme our British driver described, I understood his perspective. I have seen enough young Italians trying to impress the ladies in the piazzas who fit his description all too well. And coming from a Brit, who may be more reserved compared to the more expressive Italians, it is easy to understand why he would view it that way. Though the Brits and Italians, by reputation, might be on opposite ends of the spectrum, the "look at me" phenomenon is one we all share.

Think about it. From the clothes we wear, to our makeup and hair, to the houses we buy, and the cars we drive; yes, we too are born with the same instinct and desire to be noticed. Our attention-grabbing tendencies are no different from those of a peacock, but did you ever think about why being noticed is so important?

Just as Maslow's hierarchy of needs theory suggests, our physiological needs come first: food, water, shelter.

It begins when we are babies seeking care from our mothers. That need for attention is a survival tactic to protect us. This behavior is best illustrated by a study called the "Still Face" experiment.

A team led by Dr. Edward Tronick, a developmental psychiatrist at the University of Massachusetts in Boston, conducted the study. In the experiment, his team videotaped an infant daughter interacting with her mom. We see the daughter engaged with her mom, joyfully laughing and having a good time. She points to items around the room in attempts to seek her mom's attention, and the mom actively responds.

Then, in the midst of their play, the psychiatrist asks the mom to stop responding and instead become expressionless, merely staring at the infant for a period of two minutes. The child, seeing no response from her mother, becomes confused. She begins to make exaggerated gestures such as reaching forward and pointing again in an attempt to re-engage her mother, but the mom maintains her "still face." The longer the mother fails to respond, the more agitated the infant becomes. The baby eventually breaks into a fit and starts crying until her mom breaks the still face and begins to respond happily again.

The video clearly illustrates the child's basic need for her mother's attention, underscoring a need we all share. The research further illustrates that *connection* means more than just being physically present. The mere presence of the child's mom was not enough. The baby needed her mom's attention in some way in order for her to feel safe and "connected."

The primal thought in our brains as infants is, "If mom doesn't 'see me', and I'm not fed, I will die." This is our 1.0-version brain at work. Known as the "reptilian" brain, the amygdala (which we will examine further in chapter one), is the part of our brain that's hardwired to protect us from threats or danger of any kind.

When we are infants, not attracting attention is a real life-and-death situation. The interesting thing, though, is that the amygdala part of the brain is hardwired to understand that *connection = survival*. It's how we are programmed. And as we age and mature, that same primal need does not go away. Whether we are two, or a hundred and two, we still need that connection to feel safe.

As adults, when we don't feel a connection with others, we don't exactly start crying, but the nature of the response is the same. Have you ever experienced trying to talk to someone who is obsessively checking their cell phone? It might sound like, "Hello!! (waving hands wildly) Over here! Are you even listening to me??" Hmmm . . . seems similar to the still face, doesn't it?

It is not surprising that studies show that the happiest people, and the people who live the longest, have the strongest relationships. Your brain likes it when you're connected because that means you will be safe and survive. Simply put, your connection to others signals the brain to produce more happy chemicals, and, like an energy boost, life simply feels better and we are actually healthier when we have deep connections in our lives.

On the flip side, think of a time when you've been cut off or forgotten about. How does it feel? Isolating? Lonely? It's as if the brain has a checkbox for connection. And when the "connection" box is not checked, the brain goes on alert because it is equating this situation with a risk to your survival. No one enjoys feeling abandoned or forgotten. That is why we seek connections and like to be noticed. It simply feels better, to our brains and for our health, so we seek it out.

As individuals, our "look at me" approach may differ, as well as our reasons, but the need is the same. We may have the desire to be seen or recognized, we may be trying to overcompensate for something we lack, or we may want to be seen because we are in competition for something, such as a potential mate or a promotion in the workplace.

Whatever the need and however it is manifested, our desire to stand out is both universal and natural, and we are no different from those who have preceded us. And when it comes to the workplace, from generation to generation, our views, experiences, and/or values may differ, but the goal remains the same: achieve, compete, advance, and be recognized as a "rock star."

One of the most frequently asked questions I get from those who have been in the workplace for a few years is "How do I stand out among my peers so that I get promoted?"

If this is you, you are in the right place.

With the advent of technology, the workplace is becoming more and more competitive, thus it becomes harder and harder for emerging leaders to distinguish themselves as "rock stars" in the marketplace.

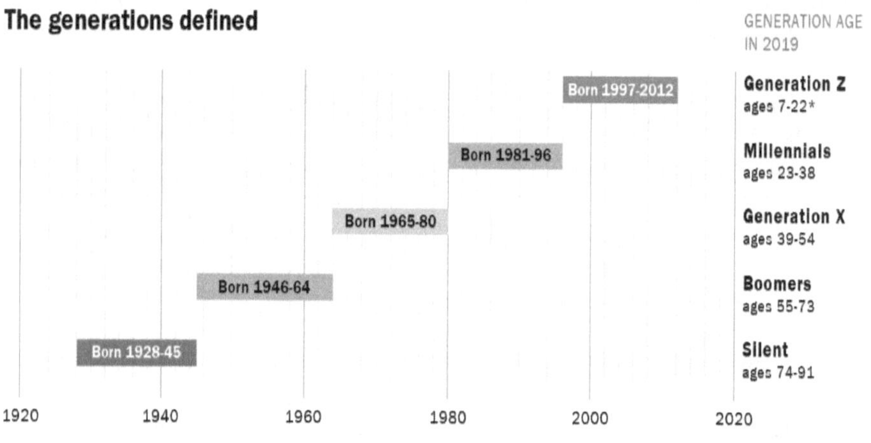

Consider this statistic: By the year 2025, Millennials and Gen Z (those coming up after Millennials) will constitute 56 percent of the workforce. In 2016, Millennials became the largest generation in the labor force, with 56 million Millennials either working or looking for work. That's a whole lotta job and promotion seekers, which may be great for employers, but for you, it's competition. And you've got to be doing something pretty unique these days to get noticed.

Since its inception, my firm, *Be Greater Consulting,* has been dedicated to helping Millennials and Gen Xers succeed in the workplace, and we've been helping employers and leaders work more effectively with those Millennials and Gen Xers. Through my work with both high performing and emerging leaders, and the organizations that employ them, I have found that there are key elements that are critical to the success of both generations. My mission is to help companies develop their people at all levels so they can reach higher levels of productivity and achieve growth faster.

Waiting until someone is near the end of their career to start coaching and developing them is not a winning formula. It is not sustainable for the company, nor is it as beneficial to the employee at that stage in their career. It is for that reason that my firm focuses on what I call "the heart of the organization" in order to build greatness from the inside, out. The focus on next generation leaders is what makes companies competitive, and helps increase retention and engagement. Our approach is to help companies and individuals develop the skills and culture to, well, be greater.

In my leadership consulting engagements I have one basic goal: to elevate the performance of my clients to "rock star" status. To do that, we focus on three critical concepts:

1. Leading self: Uncovering blind spots and increasing your self-awareness and leadership potential.
2. Leading others: Aligning intention with impact in order to motivate and influence others that work for you to perform at the highest levels.
3. Leading teams: Improving cross functional partnerships and navigating through leading without authority as well.

With those three components aligned, my clients find their inner "rock star" and their employers become the beneficiaries, which brings me to the purpose of this book:

Millennials and Gen Xers are our next-generation leaders. They are all seeking to innovate, succeed, lead, and stand out. However, many of them are operating without a roadmap or GPS. "IIow do I get there?" they ask. It can feel like being in a maze or fog where nothing is clear.

To add to the confusion, the airwaves are flooded with proposed magic formulas and quick fixes guaranteed to make one successful in the marketplace and in life. There are "Three steps to (fill in the blank)," and "Five sure-fire ways to (whatever)," but in reality, there's been little real applicable guidance for Millennials and other emerging leaders in terms of how to survive, thrive, and compete . . . let alone stand out from the crowd.

I have worked with clients who have thought they were ready for a promotion, only to be hit with a hard "no." The absence of a "playbook" takes its toll. As one of my Millennial colleagues, James, recently told me, "When you think about it, we're all kind of plucked out of college with no knowledge of how to be."

Many times, however, the employer who plucked you out of college is usually operating under the assumption that you *should* already know how to be. Therein lies the disconnect. When you do not immediately hit the ground running, your manager gets frustrated, and you get frustrated. What occurs next is a gap between where you actually are and where they expect you to be as a leader.

My goal is to help bridge that gap.

What is described in this book is an approach designed to take you and your brain from version 1.0 to 2.0—to allow you to discover your "inner CEO," or "inner rock star," if you will.

Think of the following chapters as a playbook to guide your growth and career development as a leader. Although there are no quick fixes, there are ways to approach your leadership journey that will save you time. In this way, I will help you plan and strategize tactics that will ultimately bring you the success you desire and expect for yourself. Think of it as a life hack . . . a way for you to get ahead and stay a step ahead of your peers.

However, this approach may require you to see things from a different perspective. You see, rock stars are accustomed to having the spotlight shine on them. That is normal, right? We are conditioned from birth to put the spotlight on ourselves. The "look at me" phenomenon is not only a natural one, but it's also very powerful. We all have it, even those who might characterize themselves as being "shy" or "selfless" or "egoless." It is not that they are without ego or have no ego needs. They do. But perhaps like those who are able to lead or inspire others, they have uncovered a secret about how they fulfill those needs.

Therein lies one of the greatest paradoxes of leadership.

Consider the greatest, most respected leaders you know. Their spotlight is not directed toward themselves, but toward others or toward a greater good. From Mother Teresa, to Oprah Winfrey, to Barack Obama, these leaders did not distinguish themselves by saying "Look at me!" but by serving and making connections with others. They put the spotlight on the needs of others. In doing so, they also found their life purpose (more on that later too). They shifted the spotlight away from "Look at me!" to shining it on others by asking "How can I help you?" and "How can we make a difference?"

Through this approach, successful leaders find that by helping others, their own success, money, and "rock star" status have naturally followed. They do not chase success. Success chases them.

As author and former Managing Director of Lucent Technologies, Ashok Shah states, "Those are the attributes that achieve not lifetime employment, but lifetime employability."

You see, I do not want you to just *know how others* became rock stars. I want *you to become* one. I will provide the ingredients in small, bite-sized portions with an outcome of you being ready for the mainstage. This will be your roadmap to being prepared to perform, not as a "me" leader, but by focusing on others. As educator, author, orator and advisor to presidents of the United States, Booker T. Washington once said, "If you want to lift yourself up, lift up *someone else.*"

You will learn how next-generation leaders differentiate themselves and succeed in today's workplace. You will also learn how to accelerate your own career growth, stay connected to your purpose, and work more effectively with all generations.

The fact is, your "inner rock star" already resides within you. It simply is waiting to be discovered. So, if you're ready to discover it, we'll begin where everything pertaining to human behavior begins . . . with the brain. We will start by examining the basics of what causes us to think and act the way we do, and adjust our thought process accordingly. Following that brief journey into the basics of neuroscience and human behavior, we will then sprinkle in the appropriate leadership lessons and skills, complete with drills and exercises.

This book will teach you how to achieve greatness, not by using your natural "look at me" instincts, but by employing the antithesis of "look at me" tactics. This book is about how, by serving others, you can develop the right relationships and attributes that will, in turn, make you a strong and sought-after leader.

Individuals who achieve greatness do so by how they think, how they act, and how they engage others. The way to greatness and standing out is not in the *doing*, but in the *being*.

This book shares exactly that. #begreater

Ready to rock? Let's go!
BT

Section I:

Discovering Your Inner Rock Star

1

Insane in the Brain

How to Develop Mental Flexibility, Change Habits, and Increase Leadership Skills Based on Neuroscience

Neuroscience and Your Inner Rock Star

> *"Music gives a soul to the universe, wings to the mind, flight to the imagination, and life to everything."*
>
> *-Plato*

So, what does music have to do with you and your leadership capabilities, you ask? Your leadership flows from a similar source as that of great music. It comes from a source that many people don't always understand, or know, how to access.

In the same way Plato's quote suggests, by "tuning in" to who you are as a leader, you can give purpose to the work you do, wings to your leadership capabilities, flight to your career, and life to everything.

Since we're embarking on a journey together, let's kick things off with a fundamental premise. Whether it's in a corporate long-term engagement or a one-on-one coaching session, I always tell my clients one of the first things I learned at the Coaches Training Institute, "Not a single one of you is broken. So, let's start there. You are all naturally creative, resourceful, and whole."

Ahhhhh . . . Doesn't that sound nice? That's music to my ears! So regardless of the pressure you're putting on yourself, or what your family thinks you should be doing with your life, or what your boss or co-workers think of you, it doesn't matter. You are a rock star. You just need more access to higher-level thinking, more often, so you can make great music and keep in harmony with others. We all do.

If you aren't already familiar with leadership coaching, let me tell you the best part: No judgment comes from your coach! It's a judgment-free zone. And the best part is that not only do I, as your coach, think you are creative, resourceful, and whole, but I also will always see the best in you and remind you, once again, that you are a freaking rock star. *Woot! (Feel free to air guitar as you wish!)*

In this chapter, we'll be discussing neuroscience and how your brain functions. There is actually a part of your brain that is designed to give you access to the highest levels of thinking, creative problem solving, strategic analysis, and empathy in a way you've never experienced before. And you can have it all by creating a pathway to what I refer to as your "inner rock star."

Neuroscience in Action

Before we discover more about the rock star mentality, let's look at the two parts of the brain that control our behavior.

The amygdala (pronounced ah-MIG-dah-la) is the part of your brain that develops first and is a part of your limbic system. Fun fact: the term "amygdala" is derived from the Greek word *amugdalē*, which means "almond," referring to its shape.

There are several ways the amygdala and its function have been described.

This part of the brain is most commonly referred to as your reptilian or "lizard" brain because it's the primitive part of the brain responsible for survival and is designed to protect you from threats.

This part of your brain controls your "fight-or-flight" response, which is a combination of reactions to stress. It's also the hyper-vigilant part of your brain that warns you of dangers, whether real or imagined; and *unless intercepted*, will *react* to those perceived threats. If there's one word that comes to mind with the amygdala, it's fear.

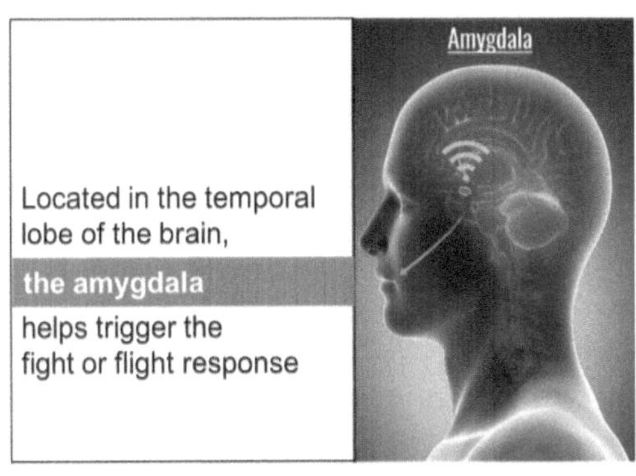

The amygdala has also been referred to as your "monkey brain" because it does tend to get a little wacky in its behavior at times.

BJ Gallagher, bestselling author and workplace expert, explains in her article, "Buddha: How to Tame Your Monkey Mind," that Buddha described the human mind as being filled with drunken monkeys jumping around, screeching, chattering, and carrying on endlessly. Buddha continued to explain that we all have monkey minds, with dozens of monkeys all clamoring for attention. Fear is an especially loud monkey, sounding the alarm incessantly, pointing out all the things we should be wary of and everything that could go wrong.

For more info on your monkey-mind brain visit the resource center at www.begreaterconsulting.com/book (Password: rockon).

Although "drunk monkey" does have an interesting visual, I prefer the more functional aspect of the role of the amygdala. In his book *Emotional Intelligence,* Daniel Goleman describes the amygdala as a neural tripwire. It's designed to look for threats and send signals of "crisis" to all parts of the body. Goleman calls these events an "amygdala hijack."

The signals Goleman refers to are hormones sent to your extremities so you can react quickly. "Marching orders" are given out and a cascade of adrenaline, testosterone, and cortisol start pumping through your body. You may have heavy breathing and muscle tension, your heart rate will start increasing, and even your face can get red at times, all in preparation to attack or to flee.

Want to see your amygdala in action? Watch a person who is scared of birds react when a tiny little bird approaches from above.

Here's where we become "insane in the brain." The amygdala does *not* have the ability to distinguish between real or perceived threats. It makes the assumption that everything stressful is life-threatening, even when it's not. That traffic jam? Your performance review? These aren't life-threatening situations, but they create anxiety. This is part of the insanity of it all. This signal of stress isn't a threat to our lives, but still floods us with cortisol and pumps huge amounts of adrenaline through the body, screaming, "Beware, threat approaching. Either go into your fighting stance or go run and hide!" And in many situations, it's a little overdramatic.

Here is an interesting example: When a zebra is being chased by a lioness, the amygdala kicks into high gear, performing as it should. But once that zebra is safe, and the coast is clear, the adrenaline and other amygdala-producing hormones dissipate immediately. Something different happens in humans. If we are constantly feeling under attack, those highly reactive hormones can stay with us for 24 hours. So when you're riled up about something at work, and you keep thinking or talking about the incident, it's because your alert signals are still keeping you in a fight-or-flight mode. And when you are not in *real* danger and your mind is still stressing about a situation, it negatively impacts your ability to lead.

The amygdala is designed to keep you out of harm's way and essentially serves as security to protect you; think of it like a bouncer at the club that looks for threats. But it also makes the call that some non-life threatening, stressful situations are threats too, when they're actually not. This reactive behavior creates a dangerous long-term situation if we don't keep our "bouncer" in check.

Determining a Threat

Your brain is like a master supercomputer. Faster than anything that currently exists today, it processes information in a fraction of a second. Imagine you hear a coworker say, "Uuhhh, I would *never* do the project *that* way." Your amygdala, positioned to retrieve inputs from what it sees and hears, receives this message and instantly searches through your entire past, like a filing cabinet, to determine if the message is simply a harmless comment, or if this type of comment has hurt you before.

Then, *bingo*! We have a match.

In sixth grade your math teacher thought you didn't know anything, that you were stupid, and that you would probably never get anything right in life. He would always ask, "Why did you do it *that* way?" So, now, when someone simply asks out of curiosity, "Why did you do it that way?," in a fraction of a second your bouncer matches the word "why" with a threatening experience, and screams, "*Threat!*"—and reacts. Your brain does not know a real threat, like a lioness chasing you down, from a perceived threat, like a non-life-threatening, yet unsettling, comment. All it sees is danger and gives you marching orders to "react!" The brain puts all of its energy and resources into your extremities for fight-or-flight mode.

When the amygdala, or your bouncer, goes into hijack mode, you do not think. I repeat. You CANNOT think properly when you are in a reactive state of stress where your bouncer has taken over.

***

An Example at Home: The Dishes, The Insanity

Michelle and Brian are roommates. Michelle is more on the messy side and doesn't think it's a big deal to leave dishes in the sink. Brian, on the other hand, has always grown up having to do all the dishes and can't understand why you'd leave dishes in the sink when the dishwasher is two seconds away. They've had multiple discussions about this, and Michelle has agreed to stop leaving them in the sink.

Brian comes home from work one day and finds a glass, a skillet, plates, and silverware, all dirty, sitting in the sink.

He becomes furious and immediately texts Michelle with a picture of the scene of the "crime":

"Are you serious?!!?" Brian asks.

"About what?" Michelle responds.

Brian continues, "Didn't we talk about the dishes?"

"I didn't leave them there that long ago," Michelle says. "What's the big deal?"

"I'm just confused. I thought we agreed to keep the sink clean," replies Brian.

"YOU like it clean, I'm ok with a few dishes . . . Soooo? AND I was in a hurry. I'll get to them when I get home, it's not a big deal," says Michelle.

"Nope, don't worry about it, already done. Later," says a beyond-frustrated Brian.

Michelle responds, "Great, thanks! Later!"

***

So let's deconstruct what's happened here. First, the amygdala sees or hears something, and that information gets checked by "security."

Amygdala asks: "Is this a threat? Do I need to alert my human?"

Amygdala quickly checks your historical "files" of things that you have experienced at any point in your life or even stories you've heard about other people, and it determines:
1. If the dishes are left in the sink it will smell. Then it considers, well, what would happen next?
2. Once it smells there will be bugs flying around. (Then what?)
3. Once there are bugs, and it sits long enough, the dirty dishes are going to attract bigger bugs like cockroaches and even rats. Gross. (Then what?)
4. If there are rodents in the house they'll come in the middle of the night, crawl over my face, bite me, and . . .
5. I'll die.

Insane in the membrane.

Upon determining this "threat," your amygdala sends an alert out to your extremities, floods you with cortisol and adrenaline, and the next step is an immediate reaction with a message: "Fire off a text immediately!"

Having dirty dishes in the sink is not a real threat to your life, but your brain actually perceives it as a risk to your life. Look at that crazy thought process. It's just not logical.

But your amygdala is operating at lightning-fast speed, and it reacts. In this case, you know that death from dirty dishes is a silly scenario that's never going to happen. You know this at a conscious level. The amygdala, however, is working behind-the-scenes at a subconscious level. Your amygdala is also in a reactive state because the connection has been lost.

Remember the "still face" experiment described in the introduction with the baby who was frustrated? As we could see, her mother was there physically, but there was no actual emotional connection going on. We knew the baby wasn't in any real danger, but because the baby perceived she had lost connection with her mother, it triggered her emotional response. Same situation here. Brian thought he was connecting with Michelle, and it turns out, he wasn't being heard.

If you ever experience a situation like this and notice you are still soooo so so mad at your roommate for not cleaning the dishes, even though it's a full day later, just remember: it's because those "high alert" chemicals can remain in your body for up to a day!!!
These situations don't just happen at home. Consider this example...

***

The Bouncer at Work: The Impact on Your Leadership

Tord is managing the implementation of a new automated system on location at a customer site. Two weeks into the project, there has already been some feedback from the customer that the implementation is "too disruptive to day-to-day operations," requiring some coaching and counseling discussions between Tord and his boss, Carrie. Carrie's message: "Take more care to be considerate and sensitive to the customer's ongoing operation during your implementation."

Tord takes the message to heart and adjusts the implementation schedule, which requires his team to remain on-site on some occasions until 10 or 11 p.m. The changes he and his team makes are a pain, but he is confident that he and his team are handling the changes well.

One morning during the implementation, Tord comes in to find he has been cc'd on an email from Carrie to the customer. The email begins:

"I realize Tord and his team have been a disruption to your operations . . ."

That's all it takes. Tord was furious.

He immediately picks up the phone to call his boss. When Carrie answers, without even acknowledging who was calling, Tord begins yelling. "We've done nothing but bust our butts for the last two weeks to be sensitive and considerate of the customer's operation like you asked us to do. We have been on site past midnight to stay out of the customer's way..."

Carrie lets Tord reach a pause to catch his breath, and then calmly asks, "Tord have you even read the email?" Tord responds angrily, "I didn't need to. I saw all I needed to see."

In a quiet tone, Carrie makes one simple request. "Please hang up and read the email in its entirety, and then call me back."

Tord is still angry, but agrees to do as his boss has asked him to do. After ending the call, Tord goes back to resume reading.

"I realize Tord and his team have been a disruption to your operations, especially in the early phase of the implementation. And I appreciate your feedback that the adjustments and sacrifice they have made to accommodate your request have made the implementation run smoothly and that you are getting good feedback from your team as well.

I will make sure that Tord and his team are well recognized for their willingness to go above and beyond their normal routine the way they have."

Much regards,

Carrie
cc: Tord

Tord takes a deep breath. Realizing that his bouncer had gotten the best of him, he reluctantly picks up his phone to call his boss, wishing there were a way he could simply say, "Never mind."

It was too late for that.

***

The amygdala is a bouncer that serves as your security. Its function is critical for our own survival, but it is potentially dangerous when it's overactive during a situation that we logically know is not life-threatening.

The element of the brain that is literally a lifesaving device for animals can be a career-ending device for us humans.

Party Like a Rock Star

Did you know that in addition to a bouncer, you have an inner rock star embedded inside of your brain? It's called the prefrontal cortex and it actually doesn't finish developing until you are anywhere from 25–30 years old. Which is why they now say your adolescence doesn't finish until your 30s. It's the executive function of your brain, the brain's "inner CEO," if you will.

Located directly behind your forehead, it's referred to as the "executive brain" because the prefrontal cortex controls many vital activities:

- Empathy
- Creativity
- Innovation
- New ideas

- Problem-solving
- Differentiating among conflicting thoughts
- Understanding one's impact on others
- Planning
- Strategic thinking
- Decision-making
- Impulse control

Your maturity lies in the prefrontal cortex as well. It's the place that has all the right answers and knows how to communicate things in a way that connects with the issue, connects with others, and brings out the best solution for everyone involved. Like a rock star.

Now, let's imagine that your brain is a high-end club. Inside, you have this inner rock star, and it's playing great music. If you want to see that rock star, how do you get inside? Who do you have to pass by first? You always have to wait in line and pass through security, aka the bouncer!

The rock star part of your brain is the prefrontal cortex, and the bouncer is the amygdala, who you'll always need to get past first.

How to Access Your Inner "Rock Star"

Any time there's a stressful situation, the bouncer is going to take over and kick into reactive mode. Yet you want to be able to handle stress and lead effectively under pressure, like a rock star, right? So what do you do in those stressful situations? How do you get past the "bouncer" to the "rock star" portion of your brain? *That **space between** is the most critical part of your leadership you will ever leverage.*

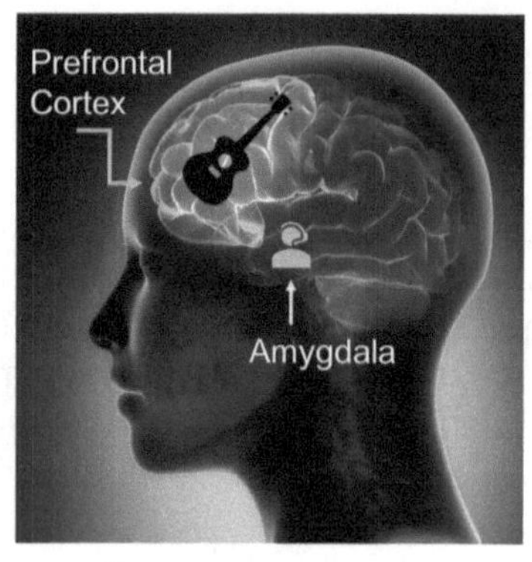

Read that again. It's that important.

It is within that space between (which is also a great Dave Matthews song, btw) what someone says or does, and what you do next, that determines if you shine. It will determine if you engage, or if you disengage. If you connect or reject. If you can master those few seconds, you will move your leadership style from reactive, which 80 percent of us are as leaders, to responsive.

Here Are Three Tips to Manage Your Bouncer:

#1: Do Not Write an Email (or Text, or Post on Social Media) When You Have Been Hijacked

Take a lap, create some distance from the event that triggered you. It's that simple. And breathe. You don't want your bouncer talking for you. Let a little distance happen and allow your rock star to do the talking.

#2: Optimize the Space Between

So now you might be wondering, "If my bouncer is always the first point of entry for everything I see and hear, and it often defaults to reactive, how do I get past the bouncer and get to the rock star part of my brain?!?" The answer is we need to give the bouncer a sedative (so to speak). How do you do that? There are a variety of methods.

The most common method, which has existed in some Eastern cultures for centuries, is meditation, which we will discuss further in the next chapter. Transcendental Meditation, which refers to "transcending," or going beyond ruminating thoughts, allows us to access a calm state where we can tap into our fullest potential. It is a practice that can give your brain instant access to its rock star, but its benefits go far beyond the workplace. Studies have consistently attributed gains in both physical and mental health, and overall quality of life, to meditation.

Millions of people have discovered the quality of life and work-related benefits of a disciplined practice of simply sitting in silence with eyes closed, for 15 to 20-minute stretches at a time. Twenty minutes out of your whole day doesn't seem like a lot of time, but sitting in silence and in a state of "mindlessness," is indeed a technique which requires both practice and discipline. And the benefits have been shown to be immeasurable.

You will have a hard time moving from reactive to responsive if you don't practice mindfulness and meditation on a continuous basis. You can't go to the gym twice a month and expect to see results. Your brain is the same way. Like any other muscle, you have to continually keep at it, in order to strengthen it. The more you focus on mediating the more you will build your "responsive" leadership.

Moving from Reactive to Responsive

Let's take a look at how choosing to react or respond can change the trajectory of the conversation.

***

Scenario #1: (Bouncer is reacting)

Tiffany has a new idea for her supervisor Christy. "I've thought of an innovative approach to get us more business with the Madison account. We bypass the project manager that we've been working with and go right to the CEO!"

"No way!" Christy replies. "That's crazy, and a good way of getting us kicked out of the account altogether. What are you thinking?!? Unreal."

Scenario #2: (Rock star response)

Tiffany says to Christy, "I've thought of an innovative approach to get us more business with the Madison account. We bypass the project manager we've been working with and go right to the CEO!"

Christy takes a deep breath in order to pause and optimize the "space between". "Hmmm, you'll have to tell me more. That typically is considered a risky move."

Tiffany further explains that the approach she is setting up means extending communication so the CEO has visibility to their work. This is something Christy is interested in, and the conversation continues to flesh out the details of what that would look like.

***

Keep in mind, reacting or responding is a choice. As Dr. Wayne Dyer states in his book, *Your Erroneous Zones: Step-by-Step Advice for Escaping the Trap of Negative Thinking and Taking Control of Your Life,* we often forget we have choices, and think, "Oh this is the way I've *always* been. I just react. I'm Italian or a quick-tempered Irish person, I can't change." Nope, nope, nope. As a coach I simply want to remind you that you *always* have a choice. Don't play the victim in this role. That doesn't serve you or your leadership potential in the situation. Think about the impact it would have on you as a leader to be able to *respond* more than you *react*. How would others see you? How would that help your career? Making the choice to focus on responsive leadership will make a positive impact on your relationships at work.

Meditation in a Minute

If you're really having a hard time finding the time, author and spiritualist Deepak Chopra, has a great video about how to meditate in as little as one minute—or even one second after a little practice. He suggests you breathe in for a count of one and out for two, and to do this for 30 seconds. Then do it the following week for 15 seconds. And eventually, with one deep breath, you can create space for your bouncer to chill. This approach optimizes that critical leadership moment and helps you provide that space between.

#3: A Strategic Time-out

Another alternative, which can provide the same benefits and access to your higher-level thinking, is having a coach. Coaching sessions usually last one hour and are conducted twice a month over six months. It is during these sessions that the individual can take what Michael O'Connor, VP of Development at the Leadership Circle, calls a "strategic time-out." The time spent in a coaching session allows you to slow down, remove the craziness and stress, and think about what is truly important. Like meditating, coaching can provide you the time you need so you can access your inner rock star, and to provide insights and higher-level thinking.

So if you find yourself in a reactive state, don't get defensive with an immediate response. You and I both know that's not going to optimize your potential. Leverage a coach to unpack some of that stress, look at things from a new perspective, and think about what's truly important.

In my coaching practice, for example, we usually look at a stressful situation or issue, and I'll ask my client:

- What is it that you'd like to know or understand by the end of the session?
    - We look at naming the topic to begin with so you are clear on what you want to walk away with at the end of the session.
- What does success look like to you in this situation?
    - By mapping out your desired outcome you have a higher likelihood of reaching success. You have to define what success looks like from the start.
- What do you want?
    - This question helps you stay out of victim mode, so instead of "shoulding" all over yourself (which sounds like another word because that's how it feels), which is more of a victim perspective, you can come from choice.

The "strategic time-out" that coaching provides is the reason leaders who have a coach excel at a faster rate. You spend one hour slowing down and a bazillion-and-one ideas come up. I can't tell you how many times a coaching call starts with "I have no idea how to . . . " and within about ten minutes, the client has a handful of options that they never considered before. All from just slowing down and giving that bouncer a sedative. This approach is key to help you reduce the stress so you can think clearly again!

So now that you know of the two parts of the brain that can have a huge impact on the way you lead, let's recap:

All the great leaders are connected to their inner rock star and you can get there too by simply starting with some of the quick tips in this chapter. You'll see that change happens fast!

One more thing . . .

When Life Happens: How to Bring Your Best Self to Work on a Bad Day

Consider when certain people or situations trigger you or set you off, and then you go back to your desk and regret what was said or how you handled the situation. Listen, 80 percent of leaders are reactive. So your bouncer took over. No big deal.

Or you may have had stuff going on at home. Your special guy or lady didn't call you when they said they would, but then you saw them checking messages on WhatsApp. You're in a reactive state to another situation in life and are bringing that 'tude to work. It's ok; you're a whole person, not just a "work person." Things outside of work will impact you inside of work.

These are the times to work that muscle, through meditation or comparable means, to calm down your amygdala-driven reactive state and find your way back to center—back to alignment and being in tune with who you really are. Your inner rock star is always there and always available to you. You just have to get past the bouncer first.

For a collection of videos, articles, and songs that connect to this chapter visit the resource center at:
www.begreaterconsulting.com/book (password: rockon).

2

This Feeling

Discovering Your Purpose

The Importance of Purpose

Just as musicians perform soundchecks before they go on stage, it's important for you to make sure that you are aligned with your purpose, and are setting the right volume, or attention, on your strengths.

Once you are living "on purpose," how do you align your purpose with your work? Determining how you discover that purpose is the topic of this chapter.

There's no greater gift than to honor your life's calling. It's why you were born. And how you become most truly alive.

-Oprah Winfrey

What Exactly is Living "On Purpose"?

Through my training at the Coaches Training Institute (CTI), I came to understand what a "life purpose" is. CTI defines it as:

> *The reason we are on this planet. It is the thing we are meant to accomplish, the gift we are meant to bring. Life purpose is not about a job or even an avocation. It is about a round-the-clock, 24-hour, every-day-of-your-life expression of who you are when you are reaching your full potential.*

It is when guitarists tune their instrument, and afterward, hear that comforting, satisfying sound once they strum the first chord. They feel and hear an instrument that is totally "in tune," as it is intended to sound, and are ready to rock. This chapter is about you tuning yourself to be totally in sync with your values. When that happens, you'll be ready to rock!

When my clients are living "on purpose," they are fulfilled. They are contributing and making a difference. When they are not living "on purpose," they feel, what I call, out of alignment. Something feels off, uncomfortable, maybe even painful at times. In this chapter, think of me as your leadership chiropractor, keeping you aligned.

If you already have found your life purpose and passion, congrats! You are rockin' it! Feel free to skip to chapter three. If not, continue on to uncover your true purpose.

This "soundcheck" discovery phase is important because when you are connected and tuned-in to what you are meant to be doing in this life, you feel most alive and full of energy. You find joy in everything: the people you are with, the work that you do. Mondays don't even suck anymore. It's really amazing. So let's get you there.

So, how do you find your purpose and live your passions every day? Though your actual path may or may not be easy, the process itself is fairly simple. Consider the following three steps:

Three Steps to Finding Your Purpose

Step 1: Connect with your own inner wisdom through mindfulness	Step 2: Discover Your Values	Step 3: Write Your Life Purpose

Step 1: Connect With Your Own Inner Wisdom Through Mindfulness

Remember the good old prefrontal cortex? That rock star portion of your brain? It houses more than just empathy and understanding. It's the 2.0 version of your brain that's more advanced than your amygdala. It helps you process information, sort out the good, better, and best, and find the right solutions. Your prefrontal cortex knows the way; you just have to be quiet long enough to let it tell you.

Slowing down can help you understand things in a deeper way. What I want is for you to be able to access that internal part of you that loves you unconditionally, always knows the answer, and is always available to you. How do we get to those answers? As we introduced in the previous chapter, it's meditation. In chapter one, you learned what meditation is and its ability to create the space for stronger leadership. Now let's look at how meditation can help you "tune in" to the topic of purpose.

Meditating on Your Life Purpose

Meditation, you say? How do I do that without taking a class or a workshop? The answer is, you *should* take a class or a workshop to truly learn this career and life-fulfilling technique. But in the interim, consider the following:

1. To consciously access this resource, find a time in your day when you can set aside 10–20 minutes to devote to pure silence. This is when you meditate on the topic of your life's purpose. The result will allow you to have a direct experience of your "true self" as a complete, loving, joyful being. This level of source consciousness involves more clarity and insight than you typically have access to.

2. During this period of absolute calm, continuously repeat the phrase "ohmmmm" silently in your head. There is a resource at the end of this chapter to also find your own mantra if you prefer. The reason you don't use actual words when you meditate is because you want your mind to become empty . . . free of thought. You are not processing or planning your day, or your week, or your life. You are letting your life plan you. Note: If your mind starts wandering, it's perfectly ok. Just notice when that happens and bring yourself back to repeating the mantra.

> "Repeating a mantra helps to transcend all mental activity, and experiences the 'source of thought,' which is said to be 'the ultimate reality of life.'"
>
> *-Aldous Huxley*

3. Concentrate only on your breathing. Breathe in through your nose and exhale through your mouth. Repeat. Shake out your shoulders and relax into the next breath.

4. Then, after a few moments, imagine you are connecting to your own inner CEO, or you can imagine it's a future version of yourself 10 years from now. Either way, you are connecting to a source that is providing you with inner wisdom.

5. Now that you are fully connected to your inner wisdom, say a few "I am" statements. This means simply saying the words "I am" and seeing what comes up. So it might start off as "I am . . . Becky," "I am . . . loyal," "I am . . . grateful." Go on for as long as you'd like to describe yourself and see what comes up.

6. Then ask your future self or, if you prefer, your inner CEO:
- What do you know about my life purpose?
- What is meant for me?
- What do you want for me?
- What do you want me to know?
- What is my path to happiness?

See what comes up. Give it time; don't rush it. Keep breathing.

If the concept of meditation is new to you, or feels a little too much, or a little too "woo-woo," consider starting with smaller bites in the following experiment.

Set a timer on your phone and try meditating for three minutes, just practicing the mantra and noticing your breathing. If you can do that for *THREE* minutes, my sense is that you will feel a slight surge of energy, clarity, and freshness that you didn't know before. That sensation is just the tip of the iceberg of the self-discovery and sense of purpose that awaits you.

From here, you can expand from three minutes on that first day, toward the ultimate commitment of 10 to 20 minutes each day. Not only can you meditate on the topic of life purpose during that time, but with consistent practice, you'll be reducing stress, connecting more and more to your own insights, and developing the ability to optimize your potential. The more you meditate, the stronger the pathway will be to your inner rock star resources. With consistent meditation, your life's purpose will find you.

Now that you've started to connect to your own inner wisdom, you are ready for Step 2.

Three Steps to Finding Your Purpose

Step 1: Connect with your own inner wisdom through mindfulness	**Step 2: Discover Your Values**	Step 3: Write Your Life Purpose

Step 2: Discover Your Values

With an ability to pause and meditate, you now have a better sense of how to connect with your energy and your own inner rock star resources. Knowing that, let's look at how that energy translates into your behaviors and actions, i.e. your values.

Think of your values like a battery life. If we use a cell phone battery for this example, imagine you are at work and have a full charge at 3:00 p.m. How do you feel? Feels good, right? No stress—kind of an exciting surprise, right? A little giddy perhaps? Now imagine you have 100 percent energy at work and it's 3:00 p.m. How nice would that be?! There is a way to get there.

How Do My Values Help Me Find My Life Purpose?

In the simplest of terms, our values create connections to others and our work. As you become more present to what you value, you'll notice that, when you're aligned to those things, your energy at work goes up. For example, if you value accomplishment, you get more energy when you achieve things. If you value connections with others, you get energy from establishing and maintaining those connections. Ultimately, our values are not right or wrong, they simply reflect what is important to each of us. It's the energy you feel when you're completely aligned with your values that tells you you're living "on purpose."

That part is relatively straightforward and simple, but there are some additional factors to consider. If someone is out of alignment with their values, it drains their battery. They find themselves getting irritated and have a hard time engaging or finishing the task. Think about work that you really don't enjoy. What do you notice when you're about to start the project? Feels draining, right? When we think about finding the work we were meant to do, being drained is a good sign that we are *not* on the right path.

***

I once had a client, I'll call him Luca, who was living overseas. He was an American working in Asia, but hated it there. He hated his job, he hated his co-workers, and he couldn't make any friends. As a result, his work ethic was getting worse, and he simply didn't care about doing a good job anymore. He was cranky, but more notably, he was stuck.

In our coaching session, we dug into his values and discovered he valued connections with others. It was an "ah-ha" moment! I asked him where he was seated in his office. He was in a corner by himself. He worked on projects by himself, as well. Of course he hated everyone and everything! He had no energy because he was not experiencing his value of connection.

His interest in work was driven in part by his sense of community with others. Thankfully we arrived at the same conclusion: in order to feel "aligned" at work again, he needed to find ways to seek out connections with others. He asked to sit among the group and requested to be part of a larger group project that the team was working on. After a few simple changes, everything else fell into place for him. He started making new friends at work and enjoyed going into the office. He didn't hate his new country or job after all; he just hadn't been fully honoring his values.

***

Once you are clear about, and aligned with, your own values, you will begin to notice that, like Luca, you relate better to people and the work that you do. You will also notice that when you honor your values it gives you energy.

My goal is for you to avoid falling into common traps that leaders fall into in the workplace. Specifically, the victim trap of thinking that they have to stay in a job. When someone is out of alignment with their values at work, they're low on energy; they feel really drained, they're in a fog, and they can't see any options.

It sounds something like this: "I'm doing well in my job, but I'm not sure if this is really what I want to be doing. I just have *no idea* what else I would do. And even if I pick something else, how will I know it will be fulfilling? I should just stay here."

What we want to avoid is being stuck in a job that we hate. Many times we create excuses just because we don't know what we'd want to do next, or don't think it's worth it to go through the hassle of changing jobs.

The real hassle is the mental energy and time-suck that happens when you dislike your work. To get up to speed in a new job takes just a few short weeks. How long have you been complaining about your current job? Months? This situation is another example of being in a "victim state." I want to ensure you're not being a victim, but that you emerge victorious in any career you choose. *Woot*!

Now, how does this happen? A little more introspection, if you will.

What if we all had that ultimate clarity about our values? And what if those values were truly ours, not our parents', or our friends', or our bosses'? That is the focus of Step 2, Discovering Your Values. Review this values worksheet in the resource center at www.begreaterconsulting.com/book (password: rockon) to see if you are clear about what is important to you. If you are already rock-solid certain about your values, review the worksheet anyway, just to confirm what you already know.

If you need help with the worksheet, consider the following questions:

1. What are the qualities you look for in your closest friends?
2. How would your friends describe you?
3. Think about the person you cannot stand to be around. What are they like? Your values are the opposite of those traits; so if they're selfish, you probably value generosity.
4. What do you like most about yourself?
5. When are you the happiest? What is going on during those moments?
6. What can you not live without?
7. What brings meaning to your life?

"Be sure to plant your feet in the right place, then stand firm."
— Abraham Lincoln

Your values are your foundation. When you have clarity about what is important to you, you have more clarity about what you enjoy doing and not doing. This clarity then gives you an easier route to finding your purpose.

If you are rating yourself low on your values, take notice. The worksheet component helps you work through the areas where you're out of alignment, so you can create an action plan to plug back in to what gives you life and energy.

Now that you have connected to inner wisdom, and found how to tune into your own internal battery charger, you are ready for Step 3.

Three Steps to Finding Your Purpose

Step 1: Connect with your own inner wisdom through mindfulness	Step 2: Discover Your Values	**Step 3: Write Your Life Purpose**

Step 3: Write Your Life Purpose

Once you spend the time to meditate and discover who you are, and combine that with discovering your values, you will get more insights on what is important to you. You are inching closer and closer to defining your life purpose.

Think about this: we all have what's called a "little a" and a "Big A" agenda. The "little a" agenda consists of our daily and/or weekly activities. We make lists. We have calendar events. We have planned activities. When people ask what is on our agenda for the week, we can generally tell them. Our "little a" is the array of tasks and activities of our current job. We may be enjoying them, we may not be. But we carry them out religiously, day in and day out. That's what our "little a" agenda looks like.

Now let's think about our "Big A" agenda. Do we have a master plan? What is our life purpose, and to what extent does our work fulfill or contribute to that purpose? Are we on a reactive journey without a plan? Are we going . . . somewhere . . . but not really understanding where we're going?

There have been many attempts and many approaches to writing a life's purpose. Some are more effective than others, and some fail miserably. They are many times a life purpose can be too specific, too work-related, and equally unrealistic. The classic example is when you try to answer the question "What will you be doing in five years?" The answer usually is "Who knows?" As much as we would like to be an executive VP in five years, there are just too many dominos that must fall perfectly in line for that to happen.

The mistake often made in attempting to chart one's course is mistaking our work ambitions for our life purpose.

If you have fallen into that trap, allow me to propose an approach that has been time-tested and proven to be successful for many accomplished leaders and entrepreneurs. It focuses not on your ambitions, but on your true sense of purpose in life. This approach begins not with a statement about your work ambitions or goals, but about your purpose in serving others.

However, there is one more equally important step: you're thinking about your future, so write it down! I am reminded of something my dad always said, "How will you know where you're going if you don't have a map?"

This process helps you draw out that map!

Allow yourself to think metaphorically for a moment and try to complete the following:

I am the ___________________ that
           (metaphor)

enables people to ______________
         (impact statement).

So essentially, it's: I am the (metaphor) that (does what?). Look back at your values, think about how your friends and family describe you, pull any insights from your meditation on the topic. If you're still not sure how to proceed, consider the following examples of life purpose statements:

- *I am the lighthouse that guides people to their dreams.*

- *I am the dynamite that transforms people's lives.*

- *I am the rock in the shoe that causes people to remember to be alive.*

- *I am the alarm clock that awakens people to their magnificence.*

The fundamental premise of this approach to achieving your life's purpose and getting clarity on what success looks like for you (in terms of money, promotions, dreams, or rock star status) is not to focus on your own ambitions, but on your service to others. How do you impact others' lives for the better? What is your metaphor in terms of your role and in terms of the impact you have on others?

These three steps—connecting with your inner wisdom through mindfulness, discovering your values, and writing your life purpose—allow you to clarify your life purpose.

The next chapter will focus on how you connect your life purpose to your career. Now that you know your passion, let's dig into how you can find work that will keep you aligned and energized. Ready?

A rewarding, fulfilling career --->

3

Imagine

Connecting Your Purpose to Your Career

Famous author and lecturer, Mark Twain, once said, "Find a job you enjoy doing and you'll never have to work a day in your life!" With all due respect to Mr. Twain, I'm going to offer a slight modification to that idea: *Find a job that honors your values, and you'll never have to work a day in your life.*

When you establish your values and get clarity on your life purpose, the question then becomes, "How do you incorporate these principles into your work? How do you ensure that your work is a reflection of your values? How do you align the two?"

In a perfect world, the best way to achieve that alignment is to first establish your values and purpose as your foundation, then find a job that aligns to who you truly are. If you have that alignment, congratulations! That means you are engaged at work, and not that many people are lucky enough to have found work they love doing. If you're in this group, you actually *enjoy* going to work and feel you are being of service to others in some meaningful way. People who love their jobs do have stress, but it's healthy stress, and it's related to addressing challenges, not to being weighed down by the problems associated with those challenges.

According to Gallup, however, only 34 percent of U.S. workers are engaged at work. So, if you don't feel that alignment between your values and your work, and if you are part of the remaining 66 percent of the workforce, then this next segment is for you.

We all have values, and our work should be in support of those values. Yet sometimes, we take a job at our own expense due to urgent matters such as needing a job, financial pressures, or other dire reasons. That is not necessarily wrong, just the reality of life. However, it is not healthy, nor conducive to becoming a rock star.

We all know that situation when we feel drained. We feel irritable, and we don't show up as our best selves. Our relationships suffer, our energy suffers, and sometimes our health suffers. It has a big impact on who we are, and worse yet, who we intend to be. Our life purpose can be very clear and explicit, but keeping those values in alignment with our jobs can be difficult to establish, and even more delicate to maintain.

So, how do we find work that is fulfilling? Consider a strengths, values, and research combination (SVR).

***

Emily worked for a Chicago public school and knew she wanted to do something different but didn't know what she wanted to do next. She approached me to help her get out of that fog and create more clarity around what else would be fulfilling for her.

I shared with her that the first critical step to clarifying a fulfilling role is to be aware of your strengths. And there are very effective tools in the marketplace that can help you do just that, beginning with CliftonStrengths from the Gallup Organization (formerly known as Strengthsfinder). Another great resource is *Your Personal Brand Workbook* by Price Waterhouse Coopers. To find out more, visit the resource center at www.begreaterconsulting.com/book password: rockon.

The book entitled *Switch*, by Chip and Dan Heath, is another interesting read as it showcases the power of focusing on the positive and why that matters in work and life.

Stay away from wanting to be the lead guitarist just because that's where the praise and notoriety is. If you're a good bassist, know your strength. Be the greatest bassist you can be, and rock it out in that role. You'll get more fans for being authentic to who you are as a result.

Emily's results showed she was high in "WOO," which stands for Winning Over Others. This was an "ah-ha" moment for Emily as she realized the best career for her was one that allowed her to engage in conversations with others on a regular basis.

She started to narrow down her search into two areas: sales and event planning (being a teacher meant she was extremely good at working with others and staying organized).

After weeks of informational interviews, she discovered that sales, or something similar to sales, was where she wanted to be. Her diligent approach allowed her to sort out which jobs she would or wouldn't like. For example, she realized that selling software would not be rewarding or fulfilling for her; if it was a sales job, it needed to be in the non-profit sector or a position where she would be helping others. Her introspection and choice to stay aligned to her values allowed her to consciously check in with herself as she explored each career to uncover which would be the most fulfilling for her.

Because Emily now had clarity, she was able to build up her network before she even started looking for specific jobs. These networks made her job search easier and allowed her to find the exact career that she was looking for. She is now a recruiter that helps others find the jobs of their dreams!

***

Very simply put, when your career and values are aligned, you are happier, more productive, more enjoyable to be around, and more successful. You've been around both types of people before, and when career and values are out of alignment, the battery life is depleted. In order to truly find work that matters, stay energized by staying true to your values and by being conscious of what fulfills you.

Finding a Career That Fulfills You

If you are struggling to figure out which career would be right for you, or want to find work that connects more to your purpose, take a closer look at Emily's path and the five steps to finding a career that fulfills you:

1. **Evaluate Your Strengths and Values:** Highlight the strengths on your CliftonStrengths report that most resonate with you and ask yourself which careers would be most interesting to explore. Review your values worksheet as well.

2. **Research:** Learn what you can about different industries. What are the emerging markets? What new industries are emerging, and what industries are in their sunset phase?

With the emergence of new technologies, companies and entire industries are undergoing a massive transformation. Ten years ago, who envisioned a reality of self-driving cars, smart toasters, or 3-D printing? Be sure to look into which jobs will or won't be automated in the future as well.

In the same vein, as you know your strengths, you must also know the marketplace, which, by the way, is in a constant state of transformation. Equal to knowing your strengths is knowing where your strengths can best be applied in today's rapidly changing world.

3. **Informational Interviews:** Reach out to 2–3 people in each field so you can learn what you like and don't like about each of them. Use an informational interview guide (for a free informational interview guide, visit the resource center at www.begreaterconsulting.com/book password: rockon) to navigate the call. Don't take more than 15 minutes of their time.

While you're conducting informational interviews, learn what those people like and don't like about their job or their industry. Once you talk to 2–3 people in each field that you are considering, you should have a better idea of what you want, and more importantly, what you don't want, to do next.

4. **Narrow down your search**: At this point you should have enough clarity to start applying for jobs. Be sure to tailor your resume to match the job descriptions you are looking for.

5. **Interview back**: During your interviews, you can also gain some invaluable insights by asking questions that correspond to your own values. If you value community, for example, ask questions like "Does this position function as part of a team, or is most of the work done autonomously?" Connecting your interview questions to what you value will also help you determine if the position is one that will energize you. Notice how you feel when you hear the answers and trust your gut.

***

Understanding Fulfillment: A Tale of Happiness

There is an interesting tale about an American tourist visiting Mexico. After docking his boat and enjoying dinner in a tiny Mexican village, the American tourist complimented the Mexican fisherman on the quality of his fish. The American asked the villager how long it took to catch them.

"Not very long," answered the Mexican.

"But then, why didn't you stay out longer and catch more?" asked the American.

The Mexican explained that his small catch was sufficient to meet his needs and those of his family.

The American asked, "But what do you do with the rest of your time?"

The Mexican stated, "I sleep late, fish a little, play with my children, and take a siesta with my wife. In the evenings, I go into the village to see my friends, have a few drinks, play the guitar, and sing a few songs. I have a full life."

The American interrupted, "I have an MBA from Harvard and I can help you! You should start by fishing longer every day. You can then sell the extra fish you catch. With the extra revenue, you can buy a bigger boat. With the extra money that the larger boat will bring, you can buy a second one, and a third one, and so on until you have an entire fleet. Instead of selling your fish to a middleman, you can negotiate directly with the processing plants and maybe even open your own plant. You can then leave this little village and move to

Mexico City, Los Angeles, or even New York City! From there you can direct your huge enterprise."

"How long would that take?" asked the Mexican.

"Twenty, perhaps twenty-five years," replied the American.

"And after that?"

"Afterwards? That's when it gets really interesting," answered the American, laughing. "When your business gets really big, you can start selling stocks and make millions!"

"Millions? Really? And after that?" asked the Mexican.

"After that, you'll be able to retire, live in a tiny village near the coast, sleep late, play with your children, catch a few fish, take a siesta with your wife, and spend your evenings drinking and enjoying your friends."

The Mexican responded, "But that's what I do now."

***

An Extra Exercise—Self Reflection and Creating the Destination

I wanted to add a bonus exercise as I think it's interesting to map out your destination. In this way, you can see what you will truly need today in order to reach the lifestyle you want in the future. Once you have done all the data collection and introspection around your values, purpose, and strengths, along with informational interviews and industry research, the next step is to dig into creating further clarity and setting goals for yourself.

One way of exploring your goals is to move *backward* in order to go forward. With your values as your foundation, and with clarity of your strengths, what might success look like for you?

65 Back™ *Vision*

Think about the goals you set—individually or institutionally. What is your time span?

Rarely do people set goals beyond five years—most often, they are for only two or three years into the future. In today's VUCA world, it is rarely done beyond a year.

It's hard to break the routine of daily life and really think about what success looks like in the future. But don't worry, there is a way to think ahead to help you today.

When we ask clients why they resist planning long-term goals, the first answer is that they can control the short-term goals. Think about it rationally. How many of your short-term goals have you succeeded in? How many New Year resolutions did you fulfill? Is this a comfortable excuse not to plan ahead?

The next popular answer is about clarity; in other words, short-term goals usually have more clarity than long term goals. When we drilled into the details even this was an inadequate excuse. Finally truth was accepted. We are afraid to look into the future. What it may hold frightens us.

The exercise 65 Back Vision is from the coaching organization Coacharya, and it was designed by its president, Ram Ramanathan. 65 Back Vision was developed to scientifically help people break free of time and space boundaries on one hand, and the consequent focus on transactional goals of money and power on the other. Money and power are important, and yet only a part of a larger whole.

As you remember, we feel most aligned when we are connected to our values. True values make us passionate. Recall from your childhood six or seven events that created great joy in you. Look for common causes. Some may have made you joyful because you achieved something significant, or were recognized publicly for an achievement, or you created something you're proud, or you served others and made them happy, or you experienced a very happy personal relationship moment. Your real values lie in these joyful incidents. List them.

The Process

Instead of working "from now to then," try working in the opposite direction.

To develop 65 Back Vision, think at least 25 years ahead (or less if you are past age 60) to a time you need not work for a living. Think beyond the metrics of wealth and power that govern you now, which in many ways limit your fulfillment. Think of the legacy you may wish to leave behind. Think of transformational leaders you wish you could be and what they think and do. In this exercise integrate your list of joyful values and positive beliefs.

Create a holistic vision of multiple segments (at least eight—see chart below) covering several essential joy-inducing factors including health, wealth, relationships, social interaction, service to others, learning, leisure activities, spiritual needs, and others to form your Wheel of Life. List two or three measurable metrics for each segment. Take time to develop this list, and involve your loved ones in co-creating this 65 Back Vision.

Where are you now in fulfillment of these metrics? What would you need to fulfill them? How would you need to change? Reflect and journal.

Use the spreadsheet format below to help you with the metrics.

65 Back Metrics

Wheel Of life	@65
Wealth	Liquid assets Fixed assets Recurring revenue
Health	I am able to ... independently I am healthy, fine and fit I exercise daily Positively worded
Relationship	Life partner Children Parents and siblings Others
Status	Position in community Reputation
Service	To community in various ways
Leisure	Sports Hobbies
Travel	Where and when
Learning	Formal Informal
Spiritual	

You can't always mandate what your life will be like next year, much less by age sixty-five, but the more you visualize what success looks like to you, the more likely that success is to occur.

> *Any action is often better than no action, especially if you have been stuck in an unhappy situation for a long time. If it is a mistake, at least you learn something, in which case it's no longer a mistake. If you remain stuck, you learn nothing.*
>
> — Eckhart Tolle,
> *The Power of Now: A Guide to Spiritual Enlightenment*

Besides the 65 back exercise, there is another option popular in the coaching world, usually referred to as a letter from your future self. Pretend it's one year into the future from the day you are writing the letter—so instead of dating the letter 9/29/19 (if that was today's date) you'd date it 9/29/20. Now address it to someone you'd normally share good news with. Write the whole letter in the past tense. Share with that person everything you've accomplished in the last year and what you're proud of. This exercise also helps you to paint the picture for short-term goals you want to accomplish, and it helps you to further clarify what's important to you.

Your next move is to find a job you love! Hint: See Chapter 4.

4

Fantastic Voyage

Choosing a Career You Love

What if, after all this work, I end up in a job I don't like?

That's the beauty of this entire process . . . there are no wrong choices. If you are in alignment with your values and your life purpose, any choice is a good one.

Have No Fear, There Is No Such Thing as a Wrong Decision

I once learned a fundamental life lesson as it relates to a career path: very few career progressions occur in a straight line, or even on a continuous upward path. Some of the most successful professionals we know moved up, and then sideways, and then up again, before they achieved their ultimate success. In each move, they learned something; something about themselves, about their industry, and about what it takes to become a rock star. As each of them would tell us, every move, no matter which direction it took them, was a critical step in their career progression. It just didn't always happen in the order they had predicted.

Feel the Fear and Do It Anyway®: How to Turn Your Fear and Indecision into Confidence and Action, written by Dr. Susan Jeffers, is one of my all-time favorite books, and one of the first books that launched my interest in coaching. And the title of the book is a motto that will serve you well as you think about life's biggest choices.

Trust Your Gut, You Will Get There

A few years back, I had an opportunity to take a job in Rome, Italy. The position was in marketing, but not in brand management (which was my focus at the time). My then recruiter flat out told me, "If you take that job in Italy, you will NEVER get a job in brand marketing again."

For two reasons, and pardon my French, I had a big "FU" waiting on the other end of the phone for him:

1. I had the strongest pull to go to Italy, which I could not explain. It was like a powerful magnet. I had other people in my life chiming in, telling me it was a mistake, that it was too risky, that I would have to take a huge pay cut, etc. They all wanted me to play it safe, but my intuition told me otherwise. And,

2. I knew my worth. I had strong brands like the National Restaurant Association, the *Chicago Tribune,* and Sara Lee on my resume, I knew I had great references from my managers, and knew I would be able to pick up a job as soon as I returned. I trusted my gut, "felt the fear," and did it anyway. I figured, "I'll just go for a year and see how it goes."

Four years later, when I finally did move back to Chicago, I was at a pivotal point in my life and had no idea what I wanted to do next. I was an adjunct professor of leadership in Italy, and loved the topic of leadership, but my background was marketing. Should I get certified as a leadership coach and pursue that career or stay in corporate marketing? What was my true path?

Dr. Jeffers' "No-Lose" model helped me make that decision.

NO-LOSE MODEL

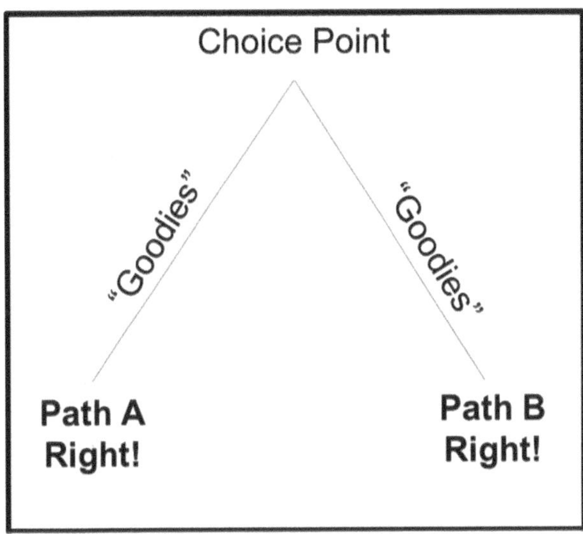

Jeffers shares that there are no right or wrong decisions. You can go down path A or path B, and either choice is right. Look at that-- there's "goodies" with either path! The reason, she explains, is that you are clearly facing a no-lose situation because each is an opportunity to experience life in a new way, to learn and grow, and to find out who you are and what you want to do in this life.

What happens to us many times is our fears (aka the bouncer) kick in. Let's say you're trying to decide between two jobs, job "A" or "B". The bouncer has to keep you safe so it wants the easy route. It then tries to figure out which job would be a threat to you, so it goes into "what if" (aka drunk monkey) mode:

What if:
- I go with job A and
  - I get a promotion in 6 months. That would be great.
  - I don't get promoted for 2 years. Then I'll be really mad.
- I go with job B and
  - I find I hate my new job and I regret not going with job A.

- I love job B, but then my position gets eliminated and I get laid off.
- The people at job B don't "get" me.
- I have to work late all the time.
- I have no say in the work that I do.
- I can never go on vacation because I'm so busy.

By this time, your head is probably spinning just reading this! This is the moment where you need to silence what Jeffers refers to as the "chatterbox" so you can get past the bouncer and think like a rock star again. To do so, keep in mind what the story you're telling yourself is, and what the truth is.

You Are What You Listen To

Remember that sixth grade math teacher who told you you'd never be any good at math? Or that English professor who commented, "This essay is excellent! You should be a writer." Or the time you were supposed to do a presentation and completely blanked out.

All of those experiences, both the good ones and the not so good ones, are stored in the recesses of our minds and are data points that create our belief system. It is that filing cabinet of old stories in our brain that collectively define how we feel about ourselves, and how we believe we will perform in a given situation.

Those "old tapes" are the voices in our heads that say either, "I'm going to give an awesome presentation!" or, "I'm going to screw this up, big time!" Whichever voice prevails is the one that is true. Scratch that. It's not actually true; it's what *feels* like the truth for you. We are, indeed, the voices in our heads that we listen to. If the voice that says, "I'm going to screw this up, big time" is your dominant voice, then you are allowing the bouncer to prevent your audience from hearing the great music that you play.

The good news is, in addition to all of the other marvels of the human brain, it is a programming device, and it follows orders. If you order your brain to pick up a pencil, it executes. When you program your brain to run faster on a certain point of the running path, the body responds. In other words, the brain receives a message and the body executes. We can choose which messages to send.

But here's the tricky part: The messages we send can be conscious, such as Robert reminding himself, "I need to remember to ask Karen out for drinks," or the messages can be subliminal, such as, "Here comes that chord again. I screw up every time I try to play that part." His brain hears both! The messages we send to the brain, both consciously and subconsciously, both positive and negative, are all received . . . and acted upon.

Here's the other good news: we have a choice! Not only can we choose our conscious messages to the brain, we can choose our subconscious messages, as well. Remember, the brain is a programming device! Just as I can program the alarm in my smartphone to go off at 6:00 a.m., I can program my brain to choose a different path that leads me to better results.

To take that concept into the round of the subconscious, we can program the messages that we hear in our heads. Rather than, "I never do well under pressure," change the message to "I excel under pressure." Or, change "I never have enough time" to "I have more than enough time!" We are what we listen to. When you say "I have more than enough time," and essentially fake it 'til you make it, you will soon find yourself actually having more time! You may get up early, create a more efficient to-do list, or work later into the night. Let your brain know what's up, and it will listen to you. It's really an amazing little trick.

And it's important to remember that the programming system functions like a muscle. You can't flip the script and expect to suddenly feel amazing under pressure or have all this time. You need to repetitively program this new thought into your brain at a conscious level, so that eventually it becomes an autopilot belief that runs on its own.

The good news keeps getting better. The brain also responds to visual images. If I visualize myself "absolutely killing it" onstage or in a meeting, my brain sees that ahead of time and is more likely to execute that visualization in the moment. Athletes use this technique all the time, as suggested by sports psychologists. When a gymnast imagines the perfect roundoff back handspring on the balance beam, for example, her brain has a clearer picture of what the ideal state looks like and can execute against that more easily.

Visualization is the means by which you program the image you want the brain to execute. It is simply a way to tune into what you want and reduce the noise. Program your inner CEO to focus on what you want and you are likely to see more ways to reach those goals. If you've ever heard of a "vision board," you might think it sounds too woo-woo. However, it's simply a visual device comprised of pictures you select to create the life you want, so that you are creating a consistent visual of what success looks like for you.

Be victorious in finding what connects to your true purpose. You are writing the script to this movie. Define and program the messages *you* want your brain to receive. As Bill Murray says in the cult comedy classic *Caddyshack*, "Be the ball!"

Now, give your bouncer a sedative, give yourself a strategic timeout, and just take a deep breath. Use the moment to get present, connect with your inner wisdom, and follow the no-lose approach. With your mind properly programmed, one of two things happen: either you'll win, or you'll learn.

Remember, too, your career doesn't have to be in a straight line. Sometimes the zigzag approach works just as well. Think of it as an exploration rather than a destination.

When in doubt, just refer back to the wisdom of Oprah who reminds us that "There are no mistakes." She continues:

> *There really aren't any. Because there is a supreme destiny, calling on your life. Your job is to feel that. Hear that. Know that. But it's all leading to the same path. There are no wrong paths. There's no such thing as failure, really. Because failure is just that thing trying to move you in another direction. So you get as much from your losses as you do from your victories. Because they are there to wake you up! When you understand that, you aren't thrown off course.*

If you get to a place where your gut is telling you, "This job doesn't feel quite right. It's not really doing anything for me," you might not be sure what to do next. Oprah recommends that "The way through the challenge is to get still and ask yourself, 'What is the next right move?' And then from that space, make the next right move. And not to be overwhelmed by it, because you know your life is bigger than that one moment."

Conclusion

The goal is to establish yourself, at work and in life, as a rock star. And for you, that road is beginning to take shape.

In Chapter one, we discussed how the brain works, including the amygdala and the prefrontal cortex, and the need for creating the space between what someone says and what you do or say next. We discussed how stress, or any signals of conflict, triggers the amygdala to go on high alert creating a "fight-or-flight" response and kicking up adrenaline and cortisol, which, in turn, shuts down our prefrontal cortex and our ability to think logically or to respond calmly.

We then discussed how the foundation of becoming a total rock star at work is not only unbridled ambition and determination but is also created by making a positive impact on others. We developed an understanding of your life's purpose, which is less about you and more about the impact you are having on others in the world. We further outlined a series of simple steps and techniques by which to determine that plan.

Finally, we explored ways to connect your life's purpose to your work, emphasizing alignment between the jobs you seek and your life's plan.

Our goal is to get access to the rock star part of the brain that thinks rationally and responds rather than reacts.

We are not there yet. In some ways, we are just beginning. But my hope is you are beginning to see the method in my madness.

Shall we continue?

One Final Note: This Is an Ongoing Process

Life and circumstances change, as do values and job opportunities. Say you are perfectly content being a sales rep for your company, and you value the constant engagement and interaction the job provides you, and the time it gives you with your family. Then, a promotional opportunity comes up that includes a bigger territory and more overnight travel. It may mean more money and more prestige with the company, but are those benefits consistent with your values?

They may be, or they may not be. Just be sure you be you.

Section II:

Fine Tuning Your Instrument and Rehearsing for the Gig

5

We Just Disagree

Reactive Leadership

There will be some days that you just might be bored. Other days, you may not feel like going to work at all. Go anyway. Remember that your job is not who you are, it's just what you're doing on the way to who you will become.

Every remedial chore, every boss who takes credit for your ideas—that is going to happen—look for the lessons because the lessons are always there. And the number one lesson I can offer you where your work is concerned is this: Become so skilled, so vigilant, so flat-out fantastic at what you do that your talent cannot be dismissed.

— Oprah Winfrey, May 2018 Commencement Speech, Annenberg School for Communications and Journalism at the University of Southern California

In this chapter we will explore reactive leadership in three ways:
1.   What Reactive Leadership Looks Like
2.   Why You Get Triggered
3.   Avoiding the Pitfalls

1. What Reactive Leadership Looks Like

So now that you've found a job that aligns with your values and life purpose, how do you remain in rock star mode at work when you have to deal with that one person that is the absolute worst? Who takes your ideas or doesn't recognize your greatness? How do you manage stressful situations with stressful people?

The Leadership Circle® has collected hundreds of thousands of responses from participants conducting self-evaluation surveys (360s) and larger culture surveys. The data show that 80 percent of leaders lead from a reactive mindset. The reason? When leaders initially start to excel, they get ahead because they can quickly react and handle situations. That reactive behavior, however, then has diminishing returns once you start managing others.

Leaders become successful because they react to things quickly and can control the process of when and how things get done. However, if a leader starts to transfer that control of the *project* to controlling *others* who are now managing the project on their team, it never goes well. If you do react to others, you are exhibiting ineffective leadership; but don't worry, you are actually in the majority. I like to remind my clients, when you find yourself reacting to what someone said, and you later regret it, it's important that you don't judge yourself. Simply be *aware* and notice the impact it has, both on you and others. The more conscious awareness you have of the impact, the less you will exhibit those behaviors in the future.

Daniel Siegel, author of *Mindsight: The New Science of Personal Transformation*, uses an interesting illustration to explain what happens in our brains when we are triggered. He describes it as "flipping one's lid," and this is what the phenomenon looks like in our brain:

Hold up the number four, and then curl your fingers down over your thumb. The four fingers folded over represent your prefrontal cortex (PFC). Further inside your brain, behind the PFC, is your amygdala, aka that over-protective bouncer. And when we get triggered, boom, the rock star is blocked, the amygdala is in boss mode, and you've flipped your lid! That's when your bouncer takes over. At this point you can say "Adios, rock star!" Your bouncer is now in charge! And as we know, that's no bueno.

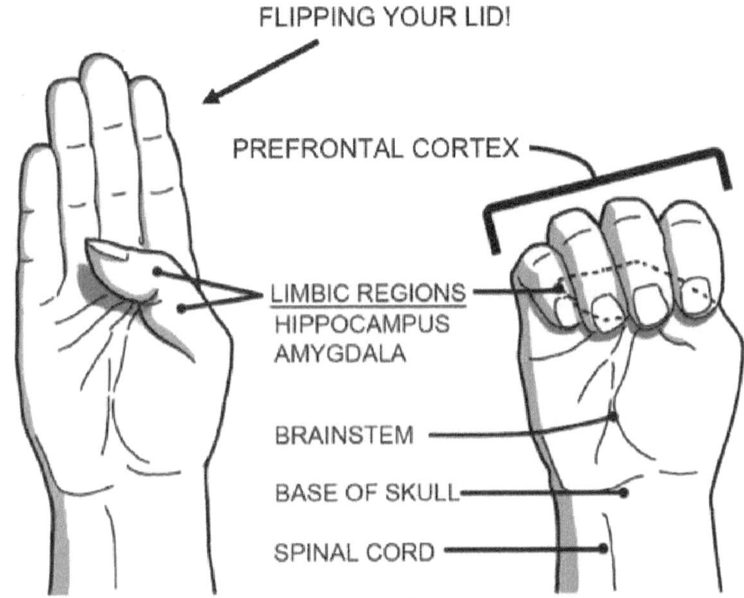

Dr. Daniel J. Siegel's "Hand Model of the Brain," as first described in Siegel, D.J. (1999). *The developing mind: Toward a neurobiology of interpersonal experience (1st ed.)*. New York, NY: Guilford Press. © 1999 Mind Your Brain, Inc., and later depicted by visual image in Siegel, D.J. (2010). *Mindsight: The new science of personal transformation*. New York, NY: Random House. © 2010 Mind Your Brain, Inc.

For a video of flipping your lid visit the resource center at www.begreaterconsulting.com/book password: rockon

A Sequence of Reactivity

As Daniel Goleman states, there's a series of events that happens when we react:

- It starts when you get triggered
- The amygdala releases a cascade of hormones, like cortisol and adrenaline, to get you out of "harm's way"
- Your brain shuts down access to thinking, empathy, and understanding

> "You can't live a positive life with a negative mind."
> — *Unknown.*

What Else Happens When We React?

We know what happens when someone reacts, and as Seigel and so many others tell us, "flipping our lid" is not only unproductive, it is also unhealthy physically! We start to experience major health issues if we are too stressed out at work—from our heart, to our stomach, to our skin. Our bodies, just like our work environments, are an ecosystem. Nothing in our body functions in isolation, and no emotionally upsetting or dysfunctional encounter takes place in our lives without negatively impacting other parts of our body. What happens in our bodies when we are triggered?

Stress impacts the following parts of the body:
- Skin
- Stomach
- Pancreas
- Immune System
- Head
- Heart
- Intestines
- Reproductive System
- Joints and Muscles

The mind-body connection is undeniable. What we say, how we say it, and how we engage others all impact our physical health. Emotions dispatch hormones and chemicals through our bodies and our organs react accordingly. It's really important to remember that your intention is *not* to raise the other person's blood pressure when you are arguing, *and* it's still happening anyway. Think about that last sentence for just a moment. We are impacting the chemicals and hormones in other people by what we say.

2. *Why You Get Triggered*

So that's what's going on when we're triggered; let's now dig into *why* we get triggered so that we can lead from a better, more responsive state.

You know that guy (or gal) in your office . . . the one that always manages to say the wrong thing at the wrong time? Like on a Monday morning? Yeah . . . *that* guy! That's going to be your test. How do you respond to that guy when he says the wrong thing, at precisely the wrong time?

He (or she) triggers you in meetings. They push back on all your great ideas. They dismiss your perspective as if it's not important. They just don't get you or see any of your greatness. You get the sense that, as research professor, author, and TED talk speaker Dr. Brené Brown says, they're "sucking on purpose, just to piss you off."

Whatever they say, it's enough to trigger you. You respond negatively or fly off the handle, and you flip your lid. And sometimes, you don't even know why! "What the . . . ? Now how did that happen?" you ponder. When you reflect on what happened you might even say, "I wasn't myself in that meeting. I was out of my mind!" Of course you weren't yourself! That was your bouncer doing all of the talking for you.

Our natural reaction in situations where we're triggered is to think negative thoughts about the other person and zing them right back. But, when you think about it, what have we gained? The opposite reaction is to clam up, walk away, and avoid the issue altogether. None of the three stress elements—fight, flight, or freeze—are going to resolve the situation or get the results that we want as leaders. Our reaction certainly won't make us look good in the eyes of onlookers.

It's important to notice when you start to feel drained by a person. You'll also notice your energy levels and tolerance for that person become minimal as well. Chances are, in the moment you feel frustrated, it's because they are simply honoring opposing values.

Know the Warning Signs

These situations usually have warning signs. Let's do a little self-reflection first and think about what may trigger you.

Consider the following example:

***

Trudy heads off to a house party. She brings her friend Will and introduces him to a lot of people at the party, and she feels like he's getting along with everyone well. The host of the party, Lionel, wants to take Trudy for a quick ride on his new motorcycle, but Will responds "Please, don't leave me!" Trudy thinks he's joking but he's not. Trudy finds herself really triggered by this and rolls her eyes. She notices that, even later the next day, it still kind of bugs her that Will couldn't just be by himself for five minutes.

***

What was the value that Trudy was honoring?______________________

What was the value Will was honoring? ______________________________

As you may have realized, one of Trudy's values is independence. And when people pull us away from our values, which are our battery life, we feel drained. Trudy had an "ah-ha" moment when she realized that *independence* was a value she was honoring in that situation and that Will was honoring his value of *connection*.

The warning sign in this scenario was a mismatch of values. Any time there's someone pushing against something that you value (such as your independence, if that's what you value), it's a warning sign that a trigger has been fired. You'll need to course correct so you don't go down the wrong, unintended path.

Knowing what drains you is important, and it's important to make sure you're not the one creating a draining situation for others as well. The more we can be conscious of what we value and not judge what others value, the more we can come to a place of understanding when someone isn't aligned to our plan.

It's Not Right or Wrong, It's Just Different

During my senior year of college I went on spring break in the Bahamas. Our hotel had very big keys that they kept for you at the front desk, so you always stopped by to retrieve your key when you got back.

Being a British-owned territory, their traffic is structured in the same fashion as England. One evening, after coming home from the bars, I started a conversation with the front desk guy.

I meandered up to the front desk, threw my elbow up on the counter, propped my head on my hand with curiosity and asked, "Why do you guys drive on the wronnnng side of the road?"

In a thick bahamian accent he replied with a smile, "It's not dee wrong side, mon, it's dee *other* side."

That's how I look at people with different perspectives, values, or opinions. They're not right or wrong . . . they're just different. So if you start to get heated, take a step back and look at what each person's perspective is. Get and stay curious about what they might value, and how that does or doesn't align with your own values. If we start from that vantage point, we have a good chance of getting beyond "reacting" to the highest performing leadership competency: "responding."

3. Avoiding the Pitfalls

> pit·fall
> ˈpit͵fôl/
> *noun*
> 1. a hidden or unsuspected danger or difficulty.

The "Rules" of the Road

Every band or musical performer that tours has a set of rules or guidelines for how they will behave while on the road. Likewise, there are similar expectations in the work world. I use the term "rules" loosely, because, obviously, there is no uniform set of rules that apply to all individuals or all companies. There is, however, a set of guidelines or principles for how to engage in a positive and constructive manner—especially if you intend to be a rock star in your work environment.

Cardinal Rule: Don't Be "That Guy" (Especially with Your Boss)

The *cardinal* rule is to never be "*that guy*" with your boss. All bosses are different, but there are a few behaviors that will put you on the blacklist with any boss.

I'm sure you don't like it when others trigger you. No one does. And if you don't optimize that "space between," and do trigger someone, it is typically not pretty. You've let your bouncer react instead of responding like the rock star leader that you are!

Being categorized as an instigator, agitator, contrarian, or obstructionist is not a good way to be perceived. It wouldn't be a bad idea to conduct a mental inventory of your behaviors and eliminate any that may provoke those adjectives.

In that context, in addition to the cardinal rule, here are two more rules of the road:

1. **Promo No-No**	2. No Skipping

Rule #1: Don't Ask for a Promotion in the First Six Months

A promotion may be important for you, but asking for it after just six months of work has a strong chance of really pissing off your boss. This issue is the most common complaint I hear from managers of new hires. This approach is a *big* no-no. I get that you have massive amounts of student debt. I get that you're living in a comparison culture where everyone seems to be excelling and making "Benjamins" left and right. But think about where the attention on that comment is focused; it's a little bit of a peacock statement, yes? You're still in the early stages of "dating," so to speak, so it's a little too accelerated for what any manager would be comfortable with.

Asking for a promotion after just six months will no doubt trigger your boss and may look something like this:

***

Rachael (employee): Hi Heather, I've been here six months and I'd like a promotion.

Heather (manager): That's nice. But, you're not ready.

Behind this simple exchange, the inner voices of the two are working overtime.

Heather's Brain:
- WTF is she thinking? A promotion in six months? Has she gone mental?
- Do you know how long I had to wait before I got a promotion?!? You have to earn your stripes in this business.
- How does she *not* know that?
- Wow, what they say is right. Millennials really think they are entitled.
- I guess she's not committed to her work if she's just going to leave if she doesn't get a promotion.
- Maybe that will happen.
- Great, maybe if she doesn't get a promotion she's going to leave. Now what am I going to do?
- She is a great worker, but she's not ready.
- This is really stressing me out.
- I want to make sure that when she is promoted, she's ready. She still has so much to learn, and I care about making sure she gets all the right experiences under her belt first before she takes the next step.

Rachael's Brain:
- Wow, I thought Heather cared about me and my growth; she didn't even want to talk about it.
- I need a boss that understands my needs.
- I cannot eat ramen for the rest of my life!!
- I know there's money in the budget, so what's the big deal?
- I'm not sure how long I can work for someone that doesn't even care about my situation.

***

Reality check: it takes 90 days to fully understand your role in a new position. Very few people ever achieve enough to warrant a promotion after six months because you're not yet an expert in your role. Take a look at the following table to see truly what an expert means:

Level	Task
Novice	Has no experience in the situations in which they are expected to perform.
Advanced Beginner	This person can demonstrate marginally acceptable performance. Knowledge is developing.
Competent	Able to demonstrate efficiency, tasks are completed within a suitable time frame with little to no assistance
Proficient	Learns from experience what typical events to expect in a given situation and how plans need to be modified in response to these events. Decision making happens faster due to experience.
Expert	Operates from a deep understanding of the total situation. Performance becomes fluid and flexible and highly proficient.

Adapted from: Benner, P. (1984). From novice to expert: Excellence and power in clinical nursing practice. Menlo Park: Addison-Wesley, pp. 13-34.

If you want to really make an impact, focus on what you can learn. Steer the conversation towards the servant leadership approach of "How can I help you, my manager?" Not many people think this way, and it takes a rock star to have the kind of conversation that shows you are interested in helping your manager succeed. The cool part? Your manager will naturally want you to succeed as well, and that promotion will happen faster than you think.

1. Promo No-No	**2. No Skipping**

Rule #2: No Skipping (AKA Triangulation)

Another surefire way to really trigger your boss is to skip them directly and go over their head.

***

Colleen is a financial planner who works for Marla. Colleen, although only 23, is confident in her capabilities and doesn't need a watchful eye from Marla to do her job.

Marla recognizes that Colleen is a top performer, but the company is new and growing, and she wants to have an open line of communication with her financial planners so she can inform the CEO as to how her team is doing.

Marla has tried to reach out to Colleen, take her to lunch, connect at happy hours. Socially, their relationship seems fine, but once they're back in the office, Colleen is very resistant to any feedback and often just does things on her own, leaving Marla in the dark. One day, as part of her manager responsibilities, Marla asks Colleen to send in a quick update on how her sales numbers are doing, and Colleen decides this is the last time.

Colleen feels her boss is becoming a little too demanding, and goes over her head to Marla's boss, Deb. She tells Deb that Marla is being unreasonable in her demands and is creating a hostile environment that prevents her from doing her job.

Colleen's Brain:
- I'm one of the top performers, why does Marla need to track my work?
- Can't she just trust me and leave me alone?
- She doesn't get it, so I'm just going to get Deb's opinion because she knows I'm good at what I do.

After hearing from Colleen, Deb then meets with Marla to discuss the issues, and Marla is shocked. Marla had no idea Colleen felt this way and is upset that Colleen didn't come to her to discuss this directly. She notices that Deb seemed to understand Colleen's perspective and is wondering if her own job is now at risk. Marla considers herself an empathetic, supportive leader that was just trying to collect information, but she doesn't know what this situation meant for her future.

Marla's Brain:
- Why in the world did Colleen go over my head?
- Why couldn't she just come to me directly?
- I've tried so hard to build a relationship with her. I get that she's a top performer, but I have to do my job too.
- Now Deb doesn't think I'm a good manager.
- This is not good for me. I'm just not even going to deal with it any more.
- Colleen can figure it out on her own.
- Wait! I can't just ice her and ignore her; I'm her boss!
- Now I'm always going to walk on eggshells around her so she doesn't go to my boss again about something I inadvertently said or did.
- This is a nightmare!

***

In the moment that Colleen triangulated, she sent an unintentional signal of "enemy" in this situation. Once Marla sensed a threat that her own job is at risk, her bouncer took over and so did ruminating thoughts. Do we think Marla will go out of her way to help Colleen and her career after Colleen triangulated?

The interesting thing about these examples is that there were a lot of thoughts about being frustrated, yet no discussion between anyone.

"Knowing is the easy part; saying it out loud is the hard part."
—*Nicholas Evans, The Horse Whisperer*

Avoiding Trigger Moments

Having candor with someone about their behavior isn't always easy. If you don't agree with your boss's behavior, rather than judge them, it's important to try and understand where your boss is coming from. And if you don't agree with what they're doing or saying, get curious about their actions. It never hurts to check in with them every so often to see what their thoughts are on your own leadership style and what you could do to help make the team even stronger.

There are invariably consequences if you are the one that triggers your boss or co-workers. When this happens, you raise the risk of provoking some type of backlash, which could negatively impact your own career. Confronting conflict is not a bad thing if you are able to hold the space where each side can use candor and share their thoughts. Confronting conflict based on assumptions and "stories" about what may or may not be true will not serve your leadership growth. Many times you can simply ask yourself, "What's the story I'm telling myself, and what's the truth?" Which helps us, as leaders, realize the intention behind the action.

As we can see in these two scenarios above, neither party was intending to destroy trust with the other person. They just weren't able to align intention and impact. Their intention was good, and yet, the way it landed was negative in terms of the impact.

If that inner dialog and frustration kick in *and* aren't addressed, things will continue to be tense between the manager and employee, which will make it difficult for either side to achieve results.

Conclusion

Our bouncer, when under stress, likes to react, which we learned can cause health issues over time. So for the sake of your health and others', it's best to align with your boss so you can avoid the pitfalls that many make early in their careers.

Specifically, if you want to get ahead:

#1 Don't ask for a promotion after only six months: Serve everyone around you and you will build your brand as a reliable leader. It's those types of trusted leaders that get promoted faster.

#2 Don't Triangulate (or skip over your boss): If you're in a state of confusion or conflict with your boss, be sure to recognize when you're in that state. Rather than react, leverage one of the top coaching qualities, candor, and have a real conversation directly with your boss about what is impacting you.

And, of course, remember the cardinal rule: don't create situations that trigger your boss. The last thing you want for your career is for them to flip their lid!

6

Ain't No Stoppin' Us Now

Responsive Leadership

Three Strategies for Responsive Leadership
1. How to Check Yo' Self
2. How to Stay on the Right Frequency
3. How to Use Coaching Skills to Get Results

So, how do you move from the current default of reactive to a default that's more responsive? How do you say what you truly want "out loud" in a way that optimizes your leadership?

When others "flip their lid," it can be a little unsettling, especially if it's face-to-face. The first thing to do is to simply notice what happens in these situations. After noticing when they flip out, what do you do next? Thinking about the impact you want to have in those situations in the future will bring the experience to a conscious level, which allows you to make changes the next time you're in a similar situation.

Consider the following scenario. . .

***

Shannon and Peter are discussing a new product launch with Peter's manager, Katie. Katie seems to be challenging every idea Shannon has. Shannon has reviewed the research, which states specifically how to increase sales based on consumer buying patterns. There is no way to argue with the research. Yet she constantly hears Katie challenging her and pushing for the project to go in another direction.

Shannon pushes back knowing that her way of doing things will positively impact sales; she is certain of this. Katie pushes back and seems to be yelling at Shannon in a way that feels degrading. Katie is "flipping her lid!," so it seems. The meeting ends, and Shannon is heated, to put it mildly.

Shannon tells Peter, "I am SO going to talk to your manager." He suggests that Shannon not confront the situation, but that isn't her way. She knows if she doesn't address it, the animosity will fester. And she never looks at these situations as confrontational. She sees them as a way to investigate and check in to see what went wrong in the meeting. Shannon takes a good three-hour break from the topic, cools down, and walks by Katie's office.

"Hey, Katie," Shannon says. "Can we talk for a minute?"

"Sure," says Katie.

"I just wanted to circle back to our conversation. I'm not sure if I read the situation correctly so I wanted to clarify a few things."

"OK, no problem, which parts?"

(Deep breath.) "Well, it could just be me, but I think I heard a tone, and I wasn't sure what that was about? Did I say something that upset you in the meeting? I got the sense that I was frustrating you."

"Oh my gosh, no, I wasn't frustrated with you. I was challenging you to push your thinking even further. I was stretching you." says Katie.

"Oh, wow. Ok, glad I asked. I guess I read it wrong then." Shannon says.

"Yeah, I wasn't upset at all, but thank you for coming to me directly to clarify! Most people when they feel that way go over my head and just talk to my boss. I really appreciate it when someone talks to me directly."

"Me too," Shannon says. "Glad we're all good."

***

Within that two-minute follow-up, Shannon took the approach of direct communication, improved her coaching skills and developed an advocate for life. Katie spoke highly of Shannon and her ability to lead on the project and continued to support Shannon's growth moving forward. Shannon took a tough situation that triggered the heck out of her and turned it into something that supported her leadership growth.

#1. How to "Check Yo' Self"

There are two things great leaders do to deal with frustration. I call it the "Check Yo' Self" method, because first of all, Ice Cube is da bomb, and secondly, he's right! You need to get your head straight first, so you don't wreck your chances of being seen as a calm, cool, collected rock star leader.

Check in with "I" Statements

Here's the key part that made Shannon an effective, coach-like leader in this situation:

Yes: I felt	Not: *You* made me (...feel like s#*t)
Yes: I noticed a tone	Not: *You* had a tone

When you are frustrated with someone else's behavior, it's helpful to reduce trigger words that spike someone's cortisol and activate their bouncer. Put all the "blame" on you, so you're saying things like:

- <u>I noticed</u>
- When <u>this was said</u>, I felt . . .
- <u>I</u> might have <u>misunderstood,</u> and
- <u>I wanted to clarify</u>
- <u>My intention was not </u>to frustrate you, and<u> I might have done that....</u>

Remove the finger-pointing of "*you* did x, y, z" and notice the impact.

Go Beyond the Story and Seek the Truth

Shannon didn't make assumptions like "Why were *you* so angry in the meeting?" She started with checking her own perspective first and realized that she needed to hear both sides to figure out what the "story" she was telling herself was, and what the "truth" was.

It's your job as a leader to notice when something is out of alignment and create an environment that's more productive. Quickly resolving situations that go south will be one of the best tools to build your leadership strength.

Use Experiences as Lessons and Grow from Them

Remember, 80 percent of leaders are reactive, so if you do react emotionally to a person or situation, you're in the majority. While that thought may be comforting, it still impacts you both physically and mentally. When it happens, the most important things to do are:

1. Don't judge yourself for it
2. Simply notice when it happens
3. Ask yourself: "What is the impact?"
4. Then reflect on where things went south and what you'd do differently next time

I, again, draw the distinction between "reacting" emotionally and "responding." The bouncer "reacts." The rock star "responds." One makes the situation worse, while the other makes it better.

So the Check Yo' Self methodology, in summary, is:
- *Check in with "I" Statements*—to take ownership and responsibility.
- *Go Beyond the Story and Seek the Truth*—ultimately ask yourself what would success look like?

- *Use Experiences as Lessons and Grow from Them*—noticing the impact you have will create a conscious thought pattern to break the reactive cycle for all involved.

The second way to increase your leadership and stay in tune with others is to regulate—which happens to also be a great song by Warren G . . . REGULAAATE!!! I digress . . .

#2. How To Stay On the Right Frequency

The second strategy for responsive leadership is a focus on alignment with others and as stated above, regulate, or be mindful of your emotions. It used to be thought that your behaviors were hardwired. Hence the old saying, "You can't teach an old dog new tricks." There was a belief that the adult brain was a physiologically static organ or became hardwired after critical developmental periods in childhood.

Due to the invention of MRIs, scientists have been able to uncover new insights about the brain. The latest research shows that our brain can create new pathways of thoughts, actions, and behaviors. The technical term is "neuroplasticity," referring to the brain's ability to reorganize itself by forming new neural connections throughout life.

As Joao Medeiros, author of the article "How to 'Game Your Brain': the Benefits of Neuroplasticity," states:

"The science of neuroplasticity illuminates the dynamic evolution of our brains throughout life, documenting how different experiences can dramatically change it. Its most pertinent insight, however, is that we can take control of such transformation."

For the YouTube video on "What is Neuroplasticity?" Visit the resource center at www.begreater.com/book (password: rockon).

We now know that you can actually rewire your brain to regulate your own thoughts, emotions, and behaviors. Research now shows that you have the tools to regulate, or turn down, the volume on reactive, default behavior, and turn up the volume on your responsive behavior. Rock star leaders are the most responsive and, thus, the most successful. So let's look further at this rewiring strategy to get you tuned in to the right frequency to get you there.

You first learned *what* meditation is from chapter one and *how* to meditate from chapter two. We can now look into the *"why"* of practicing mindfulness and meditation, and its relation to strengthening your leadership and your health.

Mindfulness Creates the Pathway to Success

The practice of meditating creates a new pathway to give you quicker access to tap into your prefrontal cortex.

Imagine you are responsible for creating a new path by walking along a trail. The path starts off kind of rocky, but the more you go down the path, the easier it is to travel down that road. Meditation makes the path to a responsive leadership style a smooth, easy lane to go down.

Think of mediation as a place where you can go to strengthen and expand your cognitive capabilities, which, to a very large extent, define who you are and determine what you are capable of.

During meditation, your brain is accessing a higher frequency, or higher vibrational level of thinking, so to speak. When it's done right, this is the state in which you have the most clarity, work best with others, and begin to exhibit the strongest leadership behaviors.

High Vibrational Frequency
(High Clarity/In the Productive Zone)

Low Vibrational Frequency
(Low Clarity/Low Productivity)

When you're in a meditative state, you can actually get to deeper levels of rest in just 20 minutes than you would from a full night's sleep.

Meditation is a very different kind of rest than sleep. It's rejuvenating and healing—as evidenced by a wide range of clinical studies—while at the same time, it allows the person to experience deeper mental states.

One of the most impressive studies was conducted at the University of California Irvine using advanced fMRI (functional magnetic resonance imaging technology). Compared to subjects who were just resting peacefully with their eyes closed, subjects who had recently been meditating were found to have an increase in blood flow in the brain's prefrontal cortex, which is associated with attention and executive functions such as decision making, reasoning, working memory, inhibition, and reward anticipation.

The study also found that people practicing Transcendental Meditation (TM) for as little as five months had more than 50 percent less reactivity to a stressful stimulus as compared to when they started practicing TM.

Meditation can help us feel well rested and energized, which in turn decreases stress and reduces anxiety. This gives us better focus and productivity, sharpens and de-clutters the mind, and makes us feel calmer and more relaxed

Connecting to this higher vibrational level of thinking is also a way for you to build, over time, the skill of responsive leadership. This "productive zone" is where you're connecting to your prefrontal cortex. The more you access this zone, the more chill you will be and the less reactive tendencies you will have.

Successful people know how to raise their own vibration to have more clarity, know how to best work with others, and create more harmony even when working with the most difficult people.

Want more proof?

Meditation: Slow Down to Pick Up Speed

A 2004 study from the University of Wisconsin took eight long-term Tibetan Buddhist practitioners of meditation and, using electrodes, monitored the patterns of electrical activity produced by their brains as they meditated. The researchers compared the brain activity of the monks to a group of novice meditators, who were taught to meditate an hour a day for one week prior to the study. In a normal meditative state, both groups were shown to have similar brain activity.

The data showed that the monks, after meditating on the topic of compassion, started to show a rhythmic, coherent pattern in their brain waves, suggesting neuronal structures were firing in harmony. In addition, their levels of thinking and processing were far greater than the novice meditators.

Based on the study of gamma waves (of which I will spare you the intricate neuro-scientific details), the oscillations in the monks' brains were the largest seen in humans. Gamma waves relate to conscious attention, meaning the monks were able to access the highest levels of thinking.

HUMAN BRAIN WAVES

Conversely, this gamma-band activity was rare among the novice meditators. Their brain activity, however, did improve over the course of the study, implying that the aptitude for one to produce gamma-band levels is trainable.

The ability to maintain that calm, meditative state, even when provoked or "triggered," is what seasoned meditators refer to as living in "harmony."

This study, like so many others, demonstrates how being accomplished in meditation allows you to access the highest brain frequency, the highest levels of thinking with empathy and understanding, as well as a greater capacity to communicate and problem-solve with others.

What you're tapping into is a level of consciousness that is always accessible and boundless. It is described by those within the TM community as being analogous to the ocean. At the top, on some days, the water is calm, and on other days, it is stormy, depending on the atmosphere. But as you sink further down, the water is always calm, regardless of what is happening above.

This is the state we want to be in—rain or shine, calm or stormy. This calm state is where you can think most clearly about what is important and what your next move is, no matter what atmospheric conditions you may encounter.

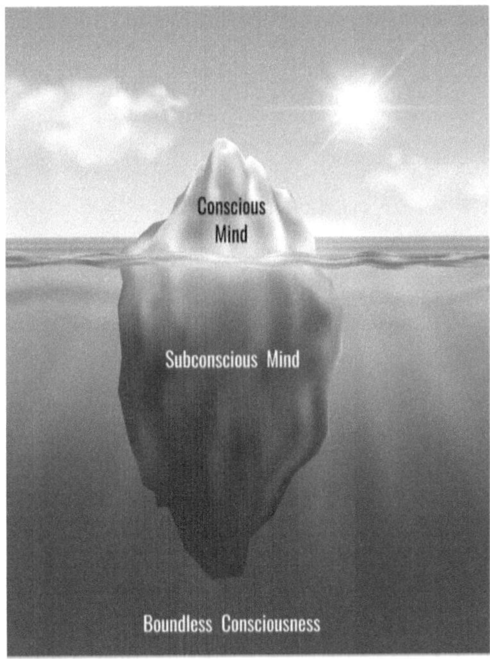

We saw the negative impact of stress on out physical wellbeing. On the flip side, meditation not only helps us activate higher level thinking to support our leadership, it also has amazing health benefits that counteract the elements of day-to-day stress as well. So, it's a double bonus! Woot!

Source: Art of Living www.theartofliving.com

So, let's test it.

Let's say someone ticks you off in a meeting because they want the project to go in a way that doesn't make any sense to you. Being proficient in meditation allows you to:

1. Hear what they have to say without being defensive.
2. Become calm and therefore able to be empathetic to their ideas and values, whether you agree with them or not.
3. Tap into your inner rock star and *respond* to their idea. Being present in the moment, and co-creating to get the best results.

As the Leadership Circle assessment verifies, great leaders are all about responding and not reacting. And once you are proficient in the art of meditation, you can learn how to respond from a state of harmony, too.

Your ability to get results will become even stronger when you apply the third strategy for responsive leadership, which is to leverage coaching skills.

#3. How to Use Coaching Skills to Get Results

The International Coach Federation has created a list of core competencies for coaches. Under the heading of "Communicating Effectively" are two skillsets you can practice: "active listening" and "powerful questioning".

Active Listening

You can ask yourself, in relation to the other person, "Can they hear me? Are we on the same frequency?"

If the answer is yes, it's go-time. You're aligned, in harmony, and making great music together.

When you're out of sync, you'll notice something different happens. You get the sense that something feels out of tune. Perhaps they get a little louder, and then you get a little louder, like that's going to help anything! Your face might get a little red, your blood pressure goes up, cortisol is rising, then adrenalin . . . ohh, yeah! It's bouncer time (cue techno music).

***

Steve and Lisa are assigned to the same team in a marketing firm. The team has been given the assignment to create a public service announcement (PSA) for one of their pro bono clients about their effort to prevent Alzheimer's disease. Though the two are working on the same team, Steve and Lisa are not particularly close, and are known to butt heads with each other on occasion. Lisa is the assistant project leader, and Steve feels she gets a little too much attention that is not necessarily warranted.

The team is having a debate about the wording of the PSA. At one point in the conversation, Steve becomes particularly emotional and animated. He then blurts out, "Dammit, this team has not heard a single word the client has said, and you all are about to blow this whole project."

While Steve is girding up for a counter-response from his embattled teammate, Lisa instead takes the wind out of his emotional balloon and turns him around at the same time. In this moment, Lisa knows that in order to inspire change she has to actively listen. She takes a pause and centers herself by taking a deep breath, which creates the space between his action and her next move.

She then calmly says, "You know, Steve may have a point. Can we hear more?"

Steve, and everyone at the table is somewhat taken aback by her mild-mannered response to his emotional outburst. If he was trying to trigger Lisa with his comment, she ignored it and calmly responded instead. As a result, Steve's whole demeanor changes, and she is able to encourage him to help create a solution.

Having been given the opportunity to further express his views, he rationally and thoughtfully outlines his opinion. When he talks, instead of looking at the group leader to make his points, he looks at Lisa. It's as if she is the one he wants to convince.

In the meeting, Lisa had not agreed or disagreed with Steve's views. She simply said to the group, "Let's listen." In the process, she heard some ideas she had not thought of, and at the same time, converted a one-time adversary into a devoted follower.

After the meeting, Steve seeks Lisa out and suggests the two work together on drafting a PSA to present to the team.

***

Be sure you're on the side of active listening so that you can become more coach-like in your approach, which will help you optimize your leadership and get results faster.

Powerful Questions

Let's take a look at what "Powerful Questions" do and don't look like:

***

Sarah (Manager): Hi Victor, what brings you to chat today?

Victor (Employee): Hi Sarah, I think I deserve a promotion.

Sarah: Mmm, ok so why do you think you deserve a promotion? You haven't been here that long.

Victor: Because, Debbie and Mark both got promotions.

Sarah: Well, this feels like a teachable moment. When a manager asks you why you deserve the promotion, they want to know what *you* did, specifically, to earn that promotion. So, what did you do specifically?

Victor: Ok, fine. I can tell you're not even open to it, so just *forget it*.

Sarah: No, that's not what I'm saying. That's not what I meant. I just want to know what your reasoning is.

Victor: Nah, just forget it.

Sarah ponders to self: How did this go south so quickly?

***

As we look at this scenario, Sarah did everything right— everything except one thing. She leveraged curiosity and empathy, two great leadership skills. She even tried to create a coachable moment with her team member: she clarified with him to get more information. Everything seemed on track, so what went wrong?

If there's one word that locks people into their bouncer, it's the word "why." The reason is because "why" carries judgment. It comes from our past experiences. Little kids use it all the time to cut others down:

"Why are you wearing THAT shirt?" "Why don't you know the answer? Are you stupid?" So "why" doesn't have a nice sound to us as adults either.

To become more coach-like ask a powerful question. My favorite formula is starting specifically with three words:

1. I'm
2. Curious
3. What . . .

Here's the replay:

***

Sarah (Manager): Hi Victor, what brings you to chat today?

Victor (Employee): Hi Sarah, I think I deserve a promotion.

Sarah: Mmm, ok so you haven't been here that long. **I'm curious, what** do you know about promotions here?

Victor: Not sure what you mean.

Sarah: Well, there's a process at organizations in general for how people get promoted—timelines, etc. What is it that you already know about this process?

***

Powerful questions help you coach through tough scenarios and situations. As we can see, Sarah's powerful coaching questions were combined with active listening to make sure the two inner rock star leaders were the ones talking, not their bouncers. This strategy diffused the tension and helped their communication so that Victor was clear on what was truly needed to be eligible for a promotion.

Staying Centered Through It All

So when we think about the three strategies to stay responsive, we not only need to check in with what the story is versus the truth, practice meditation, and use coaching skills like "I'm curious, what...?" to get results. There's one other factor that is important to consider to insure your effectiveness overall as a leader.

The *Harvard Business Review* conducted a study to determine the leadership traits that are the most inspiring to followers. Researchers found that there are many different leadership attributes that inspire people, but one seemed to stand out more than any other: centeredness.

"Centeredness" is defined as having a state of mindfulness that enables leaders to do four things: remain calm under stress, get curious, listen deeply, and remain present. When you think about it, the most centered people know exactly how to respond.

Remember how Lisa was able to work with Steve on the PSA? Her centeredness is what's inspiring to her followers and allowed her to influence Steve. This is one of the biggest benefits you will find from responding to others. Influence. Lucky for you, you already know how to stay centered by combining the right approach to connect to others and meditation!

Leaders That Respond Make a Positive Impact

Have you ever been in a work situation that had high levels of stress? Staying centered in that moment will be one of the hardest yet inevitable parts of your job as a leader. When leaders stay centered, they can resolve conflicts, deepen relationships, and build strong teams. When you get to this level of leadership you will have proven your ability to shine during the most difficult moments.

If you're watching someone at work whose behavior needs to change, you might want to avoid the issue because you don't know how to approach the topic.

As we've all experienced at one point or another, fear often stops us from doing what needs to be done.

Our fear leads to procrastination, we fail ourselves, and the poor communication and behaviors continue. In turn, our team continues to provide substandard performance, miss deadlines, engage in interpersonal conflicts, and exhibit toxic behavior. Team chemistry is disrupted, and human and company costs can run deep.

In these moments you need to make an impact to create positive change and part of that involves straightforwardness and sincerity. To maximize your impact and take your responsive leadership to the next level:

1. Know your desired outcome What do you want to accomplish—what does success look like?

2. Remain open-minded Approach others with a curious mindset and check in to make sure you're not tuning into your personal biases. Remember, as Steven Covey says, "Seek first to understand, then to be understood."

Summary

One of the most important traits of a leader is the ability to stay responsive instead of reactive. In this chapter, you first looked at how to check in with yourself before your reactive bouncer takes over. In addition, you now know that our brains are not fixed in stone, but are plastic and malleable at any age. The latest research shows that you have the power to change your thoughts and actions. In addition, the power of meditation can help you bypass the bouncer and get you VIP access to your rock star (the prefrontal cortex). The leaders that have learned how to "respond" rather than "react" to situations are constantly meditating to strengthen the connection to their inner rock star. And, by learning to leverage coaching competencies, you can formulate responses that have the right content and the right tone. It is then that you begin to truly emerge as a genuine rock star. You will naturally begin to stand out amongst your peers, not by saying "Look at me!" but by asking, "How can *I* help *you*?"

Carry on rock stars. This is just the rehearsal.

Section III:

Taking it on the Road

Up to this point, our discussion has focused on how the brain works and how the practice of meditation helps you slow down to pick up speed. This strategic timeout allows seasoned meditators and strong leaders to respond and engage appropriately, especially when they are triggered. We also looked at understanding ourselves and what motivates and drives us to succeed in work and in life.

This section is about how to employ those principles effectively by taking your leadership to the next level. It's time to amp it up and increase your chances of a promotion.

Four Ways to Differentiate Yourself . . . with Anyone, Under Any Circumstances!

You may, like many emerging leaders, still feel like you're stuck. "What if I'm not in a position of power?" you ask. "What if I'm just a backup musician with no opportunity to strut my stuff? How do I break through in these circumstances?"

The following four skill sets are essential to your ability to lead across generations and build your brand. They are the key to your rock star leadership status, no matter the differences in generations, worldviews, or titles within your organization.

These time-tested approaches to engaging others are universal traits you will find in any effective leader or CEO. Master them and you will be assured of having a leg up on any of your competition. How do you ensure your job security and promotability?

Rise to the occasion and increase your promotability by following these four simple steps:

1. Manage Yourself — Focus on Personal Leadership
2. Manage Your Relationships — Focus on Servant Leadership
3. Manage Your Manager — Focus on Followership
4. Manage Your Visibility — Focus on Thought Leadership

The Power of Four

Before we dive in I want to briefly share why it's so important to "stand up" and rise to the challenge when it comes to owning your career development.

No one else is going to do it for you!

Sounds strange, right? Like, wait . . . isn't my manager supposed to see all my good work and promote me? That's actually not how things typically work. I learned that lesson about ten years into my own work experience. I had different expectations for my own growth and learned I shouldn't be waiting for managers to promote me. As a leader, I had to own it. I had to define what success looked like for me, state my worth, have the right kind of conversations, and advocate for myself.

Think of these four strategies as not only a way to own your career development, but also as the secret sauce to differentiating yourself from your peers. The fundamental components of building your leadership skills, influence, and thought leadership will, together, create a series of "moving performances" to increase trust, increase your fan base, and help get you on the fast track for that next promotion.

So, let's look at the four chords you need to learn for this tune.

7

Man in the Mirror

Manage Yourself

This first approach of managing yourself is one you will most likely have to employ more often, especially as you're navigating your way up the organizational chart. If you are not quite yet at a higher level within your company, you can still make a name for yourself simply by focusing on your *personal leadership*.

If you've ever been on an airplane, you've heard the phrase "put your oxygen mask on first, before you assist others."

The best leaders "put their oxygen mask on first," looking internally at their own personal leadership behaviors, so they can be more effective in helping those around them.

There are multiple dimensions that make up your personal leadership, just as there are an equal number of leadership assessment tools to evaluate your leadership abilities.

My favorite assessment is from The Leadership Circle®, which measures all leadership dimensions in one comprehensive package called, *The Leadership Circle Profile*™ (www.leadershipcircle.com). This tool, which I use frequently with my clients, is considered a "360." This means you rate your competencies as well as your tendencies or thought processes. Your peers and boss rate you as well, which allows you to gain a 360-degree view of your leadership.

The tool then distinguishes those leadership attributes into two areas: The top half of the circle highlights "Creative" competencies (or what I refer to as "Responsive" competencies) that contribute to a leader's effectiveness.

The lower half of the circle maps self-limiting, "Reactive" tendencies and leadership behaviors. The Reactive tendencies emphasize caution over creating results, self-protection over productive engagement, aggression over building alignment, and control over collaboration.

If these terms sound familiar it's because we looked at examples of reactive and responsive leadership in Section II. We discussed that rock stars respond and bouncers react. Now, let's look specifically at where *you* fall on the spectrum in a little more detail.

How would others rate you on your leadership style? How would you rate yourself?

Taking a moment for self-reflection, think about the following questions as they relate to leadership.

To what extent do you:

- Relate to others in a way that brings out the best in people, groups, and organizations (*Relating*)? Do you create a caring connection and collaborate well with others?
- Focus on your own personal and professional development with a strong sense of leadership composure (*Self-Awareness*)? Do others describe you as even-keeled under pressure?

- Lead in an authentic, courageous manner (*Authenticity*)? Are you willing to take a tough stance and openly deal with difficult issues?
- Understand how your job fits within the overall strategic direction of the company (*Systems Awareness*)? Do you look at the long-term effects of your decisions and how they impact the business?
- Focus on the goal, strive to achieve results, and are decisive even when there's uncertainty (*Achieving*)? Are you a visionary that gets things done?

These competencies–Relating, Self Awareness, Authenticity, Systems Awareness, and Achieving, are responsive qualities that high-performing leaders leverage when working with others. High scores in these dimensions correlate to high levels of leadership effectiveness, and subsequently, high levels of business performance. These are the competencies that you will see showcased by rock star-level leaders.

In contrast, ask yourself to what extent do you:

- Forego your own beliefs to comply with or please your boss (*Complying*)?
- Protect your agenda or territory by remaining distant or aloof from your colleagues (*Protective*)?
- Attempt to control situations by focusing on your own success at the expense of helping your colleagues with their success (*Controlling*)? Are you a perfectionist whose demands are unrealistic?

These characteristics–Complying, Protecting, and Controlling— are reactive and can get in the way of your personal leadership. This bottom half of the circle is often showcased when your bouncer is in a reactive state.

In the example below, the raters of this client are a combination of their peers and their manager. Their collective score is shown in green. The client's self-evaluation score is represented by the solid black lines. For example, this client rated themselves high in Relating, while their team rated them low. They also think they're less controlling (50) than the team's score (70).

In a 360-degree Leadership Circle Profile, where would you fall?

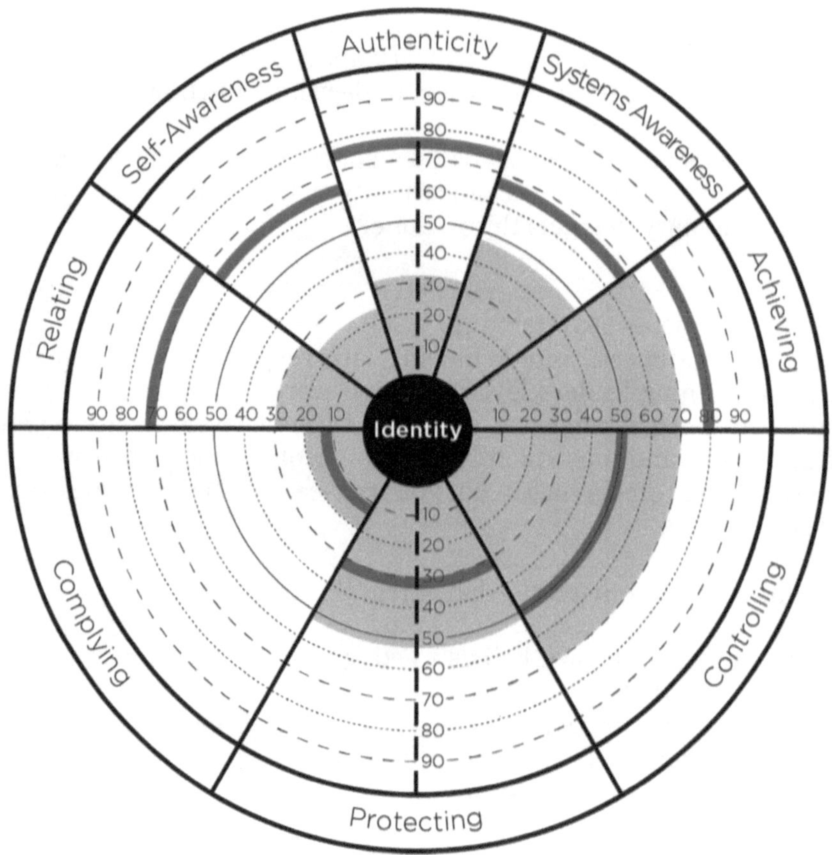

Courtesy of The Leadership Circle®, all rights reserved.

Understanding this level of insight is key. Many times we have the greatest intention to be collaborative, but we might not always land that way. Kind of like the old saying, "Beauty is in the eye of the beer-holder." Ahaha. I kid, but it's true. The labels of our leadership style are not determined by us, but by how *others* see us.

If we can't see where we land with others, we could unintentionally keep living on the bottom half of the circle. This is why having visibility to our personal leadership style is key. As we know, the best golf players still have a coach because they can't see their own swing.

We can't change what we can't see. And the best way to create positive change is to measure it. To gather this level of intel, inquire if your workplace offers 360 evaluations. If they don't, and you decide to hire a coach, request that they include one as part of your coaching package.

In the meantime, you can do a quick self-evaluation about where you think you are at, and where you'd like to be. Rate yourself on a scale of 1–10 for your current and future states. Focus on one area of strength you'd like to improve on for 100 days. Just like learning to play the guitar, you won't get better at growing your personal leadership just by thinking about it. You have to practice!

	Currently	Would Like to Be
Relating	_____	_____
Self-Awareness	_____	_____
Authenticity	_____	_____
Systems Awareness	_____	_____
Achieving	_____	_____

My one area of focus is: _______________________

My plan of action to improve on that area is: ___________

____

To further reinforce the importance of personal leadership, do yourself a favor and read executive coach, speaker, and author Marshall Goldsmith's best-seller, *What Got You Here Won't Get You There: How Successful People Become Even More Successful*. It serves as an essential guide to help you eliminate your dysfunctions and move to where you want to go. In it, Goldsmith cites a variety of powerful, charismatic leaders whose careers were going straight up, but who made simple blunders that virtually derailed each of them.

These were not organizational or strategic blunders, he says, but simple, engagement-related blunders in how they communicated and worked with others. In a number of instances, he describes faux pas by men and women who had worked hard for years to reach the upper levels of leadership and management. These are intelligent, skilled, and charismatic leaders, he says, of which only a few will ever reach the pinnacle due to small, "transactional flaws" in the way they engage others. He cites examples of flaws, such as not saying thank you or talking too much about themselves. These are things, Goldsmith says, that can lead to negative perceptions within your network that are capable of derailing the career of any leader. Understanding these lessons early on will have a return on your efforts of rock-star level proportions.

Chapter Resource:

For a free self-assessment, visit the Leadership Circle website at www.leadershipcircle.com

8

Count on Me

Manage Your Relationships

Now that we have our own leadership competencies in check, we move our focus to others with servant leadership. The mere phrase "servant leadership" conjures up what is seemingly a contradiction in terms, such as "jumbo shrimp" or a "new classic." How does one be a servant, and at the same time, lead? On the surface, it doesn't seem to make sense.

However, if you recall from our discussion in chapter two, if you have clarity about your purpose, your focus naturally will shift from "Look at me!" to "How can I serve others?" And this perfectly describes the concept of servant leadership.

The phrase "servant leadership" was coined by a man named Robert K. Greenleaf. It first appeared in an essay he wrote in 1970, entitled "The Servant as Leader." In that essay, Greenleaf said,

> "The servant-leader is servant first . . . It begins with the natural feeling that one's primary focus is to serve; then lead."

That person, Greenleaf says, is very different from one whose focus is to lead first.

For more on Servant Leadership, visit the resource center at www.begreaterconsulting.com/book (password: rockon).

The leader-first and servant-first leadership styles are on opposite ends of the spectrum with different shades and blends in between. We all reside somewhere on that spectrum, leaning in one direction or the other.

So, what does all of this have to do with business, leadership, productivity, and getting results? Why does it matter if I'm a servant leader?

How Servant Leadership Improves Your Personal Brand

Hate to say it, but people are sizing you up from the minute they meet you. The judgments come fast as people are assessing you:

- Are you an ally or a potential rival or threat?
- Are you competent or not?
- Are you someone that can be relied on or not?

In each case, your job is to convince them of the former—that they can rely on you, as a colleague, as a subordinate, and as a leader.

As you think about building your network with those inside the organization, be curious and eager to learn from others. Start these relationships from the moment you walk in the door and you will form strong, supportive alliances from the get-go.

Let's now take a strategic look at how practicing good servant leadership with your manager can help your own career.

Working well with your manager is a little like sales—you have to put yourself in their shoes. Think of your boss as your customer; what's important to them? Have you ever thought about things from their perspective? What keeps them up at night and how might you be able to alleviate some of that stress?

The key is having your boss look to *you* as their "go-to" person. Because the more you fill that role, the quicker they will "go-to" you when there's a new position open for promotion.

What Does Servant Leadership Look Like?

Even at a young age, servant leadership can be leveraged to provide both career advancement and long-term freedom. Let's explore the case of a twenty-two-year-old woman who was thrust into what is considered one of the last bastions of a macho work environment and asked to supervise men and women twice her age with ten times the experience.

Linda LaBelle, senior manager of supply chain integration for Tropicana/Premium Nutrition, began her career in a manufacturing plant right out of college. She soon found herself supervising others, mostly men, who were twice her age and with ten times the experience. Many of the production employees had worked in the plant longer than she had been alive! So, how does a fresh college graduate supervise others in that situation?

When asked how she was able to successfully navigate the situation, she said she found herself employing a variety of practices which had little to do with *managing* and more to do with *engaging*. Here's how she describes it:

> *First, I made no attempt to suggest I had all the answers. I made it a point to let them know I respected their years of experience and wanted to learn from them. I respected their experience, but I also respected them as individuals.*
>
> *Secondly, I knew if I were to gain their trust, I would not only have to deliver on my commitments but would have to go above and*

> *beyond to let them know I had their back. I wanted them to know I was working to represent their interests, not my own.*

Sound familiar?

Linda said as time passed and she began to gain their trust, she found that they not only trusted her, but they also began to *rely* on her.

> *The more I delivered on my commitments, the more they looked to me for guidance. I didn't know the concept of servant leadership back then, but that was what I was doing. I was serving them and their needs, and, in turn, they were serving me and mine.*
>
> *Soon I was developing a trusted network around me, mostly from what I know today to be called servant leadership, and following up on my commitments. Additionally, the practice seemed to have a reciprocal effect. The more they responded positively to my focus on them, the more I wanted to do for them. It was if I wanted to pay it forward so to speak. There seemed to be a sort of magical affect in my paying attention to them rather than myself.*

Servant Leadership Provides Freedom

Linda LaBelle took the power of servant leadership one step further. She described her experience when the manufacturing downturn led to her and many others being laid off, and what happened next.

> *How did focusing on others pay off, you ask? I was laid off and my husband said, "Let's buy a van and travel!" So, we did that for a year. When I returned, the company rehired me. Twelve years went by, and by that time, my husband and I had two children. So, we decided to take some time off to travel with our children. We worked in*

our community, on our house, and all the other things you do with time away from work.

My husband and I call it the ten-year plan, though it may be closer to every twelve years. Eventually, my co-workers called and asked if I was ready to come back to work. I started with a small project for them and eventually was hired back again.

In telling this story, Linda describes how the practice of her unknowing servant leadership transformed her career from a twenty-two-year-old with virtually no experience to a valued commodity as a leader. Rather than her calling her company to seek employment, her company was calling her.

How would you have handled that or a similar situation? When others think of you and your personal "brand," what comes to mind? Are you the go-to? Are you putting yourself first or others first? And how often?

If you have room to grow in the serving others area, here's a quick way to increase your servant leadership. And it doesn't begin and end with just your manager:

Select a group of team members that are in three buckets:
    a. Your manager
    b. Those that work with you
    c. Those that work for you (if applicable)

And practice the principles of servant leadership with each person.

So, for a cross-functional partner, it might sound like this. . .

*****

Allison works in the Supply Chain department and Tom works in the Regulatory department of a large consumer packaged goods firm.

"Hi Tom!" says Allison. "I like to connect every so often just to make sure you have what you need. I'm curious, is there any additional support you need on this project that we haven't discussed yet?"

"Wow, thanks for asking!" says Tom. "There's one question I've had on this project that I haven't been able to track down an answer to. Could you help me with that by any chance?"

"Of course," says Allison. "Besides helping you with this one inquiry, is there anything on my end that I can do that would help make things easier for you?"

"Actually, now that you mention it, I feel like we're slipping on the project timeline. I'm not sure why that is. Maybe you and I can brainstorm on how to get things back on track so we can all get this done in time for the VP?"

"Sure thing!" says Allison.

***

Then "rinse and repeat" this process for your direct reports and for your manager. It's as easy as that; and now that you're starting to create a good vibration, others will start singing your tune about how helpful you are.

So now that your team has awareness of what a rock star you are, the next step is to become their favorite song!

How to Build Awareness in Your Rock Star Brand

When you think about your favorite song, what happens? You light up! It makes you happy; you might even want to dance. What would happen if others had this reaction when given the opportunity to work with you?

Let's make that happen! By blending your personal leadership and servant leadership approach, you've created a solid foundation as a leader. Now let's make sure you're on track to build upon that brand so that others in the company know who you are and what you stand for.

Why is building awareness important, you ask? If you have no brand awareness, others might think of your brand as "adequate."

For example, let's think about Nike. What words come to mind? Athleticism, technology, marketing, powerful, etc.

When your manager is thinking of a rock star employee that they want to promote, they think about the characteristics of that person's brand—a key player, drives results, cares about their team, strategic, collaborative, etc.

Which leader would your boss be more likely to promote? The one whose focus is all about what they want and doing things their own way? Or, the servant leader whose focus is always on asking others, "How can I help you?" When you serve others, you will ultimately start building your brand in the best way possible and get the benefit for your own career long-term.

Don't know how to connect with your boss and find out what they need? Here's one way to find out:

Check out the ten things every working person absolutely, positively needs to know about their boss and visit the resource center at www.begreaterconsulting.com/book (password: rockon).

Servant Leaders Ask: "How Can I Help You?"
No Matter What the Title

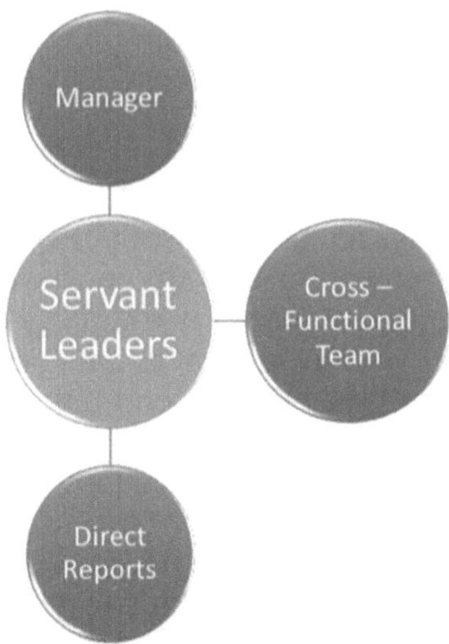

Outside of asking how you can help someone, here are a few other things you can do that will help you stand out as a servant leader:

- Align what you do at work to support the things that your boss thinks are important—it goes a long way.
- Think about other people. A lot.
  - Remember, servant leadership is about helping anyone at any level. The more positivity and awareness you can bring to your brand, the better.
- Don't be a kiss-ass.
  - Be different than everyone else in the way that you support your manager. Think strategically about what it looks like to serve members of your team and do it with authenticity.
- Be the brand that's known as a rock star at work.
  - Look at other strongly branded employees at your company. Find out how they stay consistently strong in their performance and how they connect with others. Think about how you can stay authentic to who you are *and* incorporate some best practices.

Building Momentum Through Servant Leadership

Effective leaders in today's organizations know two things:
(1) Leadership is about getting results; and
(2) Your results are dependent on your team's ability to do their jobs.

One of the hardest things for leaders to do is to keep people consistently engaged in the work they are doing. That's why it's important to remember that the more you do for others, the more they'll keep things on track for your projects. If you are able to serve your manager, your cross-functional team, and your direct reports, you will be one of the most differentiated leaders in the company. In addition, you will have an easier time getting buy-in, which is essential to what leadership is all about: getting results.

In the past, organizational charts were very hierarchical, and many leaders used their position or title to get things done, also known as "positional power". With the flatter organizational structure these days, positional power isn't effective anymore. As such, the concept of the servant leadership model is not only becoming more prevalent, it is becoming essential to helping you build all the relationships you need in order to successfully demonstrate you're ready for that promotion! Woot!

As you navigate the road to rock stardom, your ability to embody servant leadership is essential. Let's finish up this section by putting the theory into action.

Exercise:
What are three ways you can help those that you do not report to? These could be people who work for you or people in other departments.

Who: How I Will Support Them?   By When?

1. ______________ ________________________________ ______________

2. ______________ ________________________________ ______________

3. ______________ ________________________________ ______________

9
Follow Through

Manage Your Manager

This chapter will discuss how to get the most out of your relationship with your manager by setting the stage for strong followership. But before we begin our discussion on following others, I want to talk a little bit about what it means to focus on managing up so you can incorporate that approach into your followership.

managing up
\ 'ma-nij-ing up\
verb
1.	Being the most effective employee you can be, creating value for your boss and your company

As Justin Reynolds, contributor to Tiny Pulse, states in his article "What Does it Mean to Manage Up?":

For the most part, employees expect to take direction from their managers. But anyone who's ever worked for a boss who is disorganized, scatterbrained, or simply overworked knows how difficult it can be to figure out exactly what's expected of them.

When your manager is particularly swamped—or, unfortunately, like a significant majority of other bosses, simply disengaged—tackling your job responsibilities can be a bit tricky if for no other reason than you might not know precisely what they are.

If you find yourself in such a situation, you generally have two options: You can either grit your teeth and try to endure the uncertainty, or you can try your hand at "managing up"—a concept that's generated increasing attention over the last several years.

Perhaps the most important skill to master is figuring out how to be a genuine source of help. So let's look to followership as the approach to managing up in the right way.

How to Follow in Order to Lead

Marc and Samantha Hurwitz, strong advocates of the concept of followership, co-authored a book entitled, *Leadership is Half the Story*. In it, they say followership is essential to the success of any organization, defining the concept as:

> *An intentional practice on the part of a subordinate to enhance the interchange between the follower and the leader.*

***

Jeff is a director for a software company. Audra holds a similar position for a rival company. When their two companies announce a merger, it becomes immediately apparent that one of the two directors will have to go. Fortunately, a decision is made by the chief operating officer, Kasia, to appoint Audra as the VP, and Jeff one step below, at the director level. After the merger, the three have a good discussion and Jeff decides he could comfortably work for and support Audra. Though disappointed, Jeff is determined to make the situation work.

Having drinks one night after work with some of his closest colleagues, Jeff is asked how he feels about being "demoted" and now working for a former peer. His answer is clear and revealing: "I have always had respect for Audra's abilities and I felt comfortable with her. Further, I was excited about the merger and wanted to be a part of it. So, really it was an easy choice. Rather than step away, I was determined to make us a successful team. Besides, I think this is an opportunity for me to support Audra and Kasia and really make an impact."

Jeff is embracing the concept of "followership," simply defined as a determination to work toward making your boss, and therefore your company, successful.

As the company continues to expand, Kasia takes note of Jeff's positive approach to supporting Audra. His servant leadership, combined with his skill level, contributes to his promotion to the VP of another division where he will be launching a new product line the following year.

***

Bottom line to all you emerging rock stars out there: If you want to get on the fast track of gaining the confidence of your boss and standing out among your peers, dedicate yourself to *their* success.

So, how do you do that, you might ask?

Hurwitz and Hurwitz describe the following actions as essential to good followership:

1. Provide input that adds value to decisions, even knowing they're not your decisions to make.
2. Take initiative for your own engagement, development, and on-the-job performance.
3. Keep your boss informed.
4. Understand how your boss works and work accordingly.

Author and motivational speaker Ira Chaleff takes followership even further, by urging subordinates to become bold with their bosses. In his book, *The Courageous Follower*, Chaleff discusses the importance of assuming responsibility as if you own the organization. Take on the hard work, as if your own money was tied up in the company. Followership is not being a "yes man." It is knowing how the role balances both supporting and challenging the leader. In fact, Chaleff states that great followers have the courage to relay tough messages when policies or processes are not right or have room to improve in order to help the whole team succeed.

In summary:

- Follow with the intent to make the organization better
- Create efficiencies for your boss
- Streamline processes
- Take things off your boss's plate
- Ask what else you can do to help the team get results

And remember, followership is not about being a kiss-ass. It's about coming into the team with the spirit of "we." Just as synergy is essential between the drummer, the bassist, and the lead guitarist in order to create harmony, it is equally so between boss and subordinate.

If you want to stay on that fast track to rock stardom, make it known to your boss that you can be an excellent follower.

Exercise: What are the next three things you will do to practice followership? (Hint: see summary for ideas.)

What: For Whom: by When:

1. _____________   _____________   __________
2. _____________   _____________   __________
3. _____________   _____________   __________

Managing Up: How to Fast Track Your Success

As we continue to look through these first three ways to differentiate yourself as a leader, let's also think of how to best work with your manager even when you're not getting exactly what you need from them. This approach, as mentioned, is called "managing up."

As I noted previously, the leadership structure in many companies has changed, and if you happen to be working with a manager who is operating in the old structure of what's called "positional power," where they use their title to tell you what to do, you'll need to figure out how to operate in their world even though they're working in an outdated version of the leadership model.

According to the 2016 Gallup Study "How Millennials Want to Work and Live":

> *Millennials don't want bosses—they want coaches. The role of an old-style boss is command and control. Millennials care about having managers who can coach them, who value them as both people and employees, and who help them understand and build their strengths.*

You might share this viewpoint. I agree, it sounds great to have the kind of manager that coaches you and builds your strengths! And the missing Gen X link is: Gen X managers were not trained to be coaches!

It was very rare that companies invested in coaching for younger managers back in the day because it was only offered as a privilege to senior level executives. So there simply was no resource available for new leaders to learn how to coach. It has only been in the last few years that we've seen coaching slowly start to become accessible across all levels.

So if your manager is not filling the role of coach, how do you manage yourself within that dynamic?

In these situations, when managers serve as bosses (old school), rather than coaches (modern leadership), you will need to do a little more navigating and make a bigger attempt to understand where they're coming from.

This approach starts with the understanding that:

1. You can't control the behavior of others.
2. You can only focus on what you can control. Your personal leadership approach is key in figuring out how you want to lead with this style of manager.
3. Servant leadership and followership are the best ways to adapt to a manager who is operating under positional power.

Before we move on, let's look at the "payback," so to speak, of combining the three pillars you just learned.

Earning the Love: Filling the Bank Account of Trust

When you think about a bank account: mo' money fills up the account, and withdrawals drain the account. Simple, right? Relationships with anyone in your life are like a bank account as well. You can either connect with your manager, and fill up their account by making deposits, or you want to get something from your manager by taking withdrawals, which drains the account over time.

When it comes to working with your manager, the more you start understanding what's important to them, the more "deposits" you will make in their "bank account" of trust.

Withdrawals:
- Asking for a promotion after six months
- Asking to work from home when everyone else is often in the office
- Getting mad that your boss doesn't think you performed well in the last meeting

Deposits:
- Asking your boss if there are additional projects that you can help them with
- Pitching in and going the extra mile when the team is up against a tight deadline
- Asking your boss to share with you additional context around their feedback of your performance and find out what you can do better moving forward

The secret to differentiating yourself as a leader is to learn and master ways you can fill up your manager's trust "account": servant leadership and followership are the most lucrative currencies to do so.

The more you fill your manager with trust in you, making sure they know you will have their back if they need you, the more they'll involve you with the type of work opportunities that get you promoted. Ca-ching!

Resources:
For those that want to learn more about Followership, check out the Followership conference: www.followershipconference.com.

10

All Eyez on Me

Manage Your Visibility

Thought Leadership

We started with introspection about your own leadership style, looked into best practices for working with people at all levels, and explored how to manage your manager in order to help set you apart. This next and final component is about leading in a different way— through your thoughts and insights about the work that you do.

You work hard and spend hours making sure your work and projects are done well. But how do you really add value? Is your value only measured by the amount of work you can produce? No, of course not! Powerful leaders learn to be more strategic in their thinking and take their ideas to a larger audience. In this section you will:

- Learn how to connect the dots and establish your point of view to connect your work to a bigger vision.
- Learn to give voice to your ideas, inspire others, and be known as the go-to in your field.

What Is Thought Leadership?

A thought leader is an individual or firm that is recognized as an authority in a specialized field and whose expertise is sought and often rewarded. The modern-day term was used in 1994 by Joel Kurtzman, editor-in-chief of the Booz & Co magazine *Strategy & Business*. He used it to describe business ideas that merited attention.

Daniel W. Drezner, author of *The Ideas Industry*, states that thought leaders are "creators" who have two qualities beneficiaries like: "They have a positive idea for change and the conviction that they can make a difference."

Gerri Knilans, author of the article "Thought Leadership: What It Is and Why it is Important" takes it to another level by looking into the essence of what makes a strong thought leader:

- **Visionary**—someone who thinks beyond today and looks at what's possible in the future; someone who considers "blue sky" strategy, and is innovative, insightful, and imaginative.
- **Change Agent**—someone who facilitates meaningful transformation; someone who defines a goal, puts together a plan, collaborates with others, and oversees implementation.
- **Lifelong Learner**—someone who participates in self-education by reading, attending workshops and conferences, writing, asking questions, listening to responses; and someone who is motivated to learn and achieve more throughout their life.
- **Effective Communicator**—someone who not only has something of value to say, but can also tell a *story* in a way that motivates and/or challenges others to participate in a dialogue, become more engaged at work, and boost their performance.

The key is not to write just for the sake of writing. The objective of thought leadership is to establish yourself as an authority within your industry. This creates more eyeballs on your "brand," so to speak, so that your rock star leadership is building a fan base as you build your career.

Why is Thought Leadership So Important Today?

Being a thought leader is more than just being an expert in your field or area of specialization. It also requires that you are an innovator and a cutting-edge thinker. It's these types of leaders who get promoted faster because they are sharing knowledge and helping others advance in their knowledge as well. You need to always be looking forward, not backward. When people turn to thought leaders, it is to discover the next big thing or a new perspective on a current trend, not for regurgitated, recycled ideas.

Benefits of Thought Leadership

Becoming a thought leader has a multiplier effect by helping you become significantly more successful. And it's important to recognize that just about *anyone* can become more accomplished by becoming a thought leader.

Unexpected Thought Leadership

Let's talk about Dr. Brené Brown for a moment. Brown has one of the top-ten Ted Talks with more than 37 million views. She covers the bases of being a visionary, a life-long learner (she's a research professor too), an effective communicator, and a change agent. She speaks on the topic of vulnerability, and she was, in fact, vulnerable in what she shared. Her authenticity during her Ted Talk, along with her storytelling capabilities, have advanced her into Oprah-level thought leadership. She is now partnering with the OWN network to provide content for their viewers. You can't get bigger than that. And I'm guessing that wasn't her intention when she started. She was truly sharing what she learned from her research. That's the key: creating thought leadership content from your values is what will connect you with others who share the same perspective. This "tribe" will find your information useful and share it with others, which will connect you to more like-minded people that you can impact.

Thought leadership can cover anything from personal eating habits like "trends in protein" or "the power of kale;" to niche marketing like "marketing to moms;" to mental health "work/life integration" and mindfulness; to traditional corporate leadership areas such as "the customer experience," "how to sell without being salesy," leadership, etc.

If you don't have any thought leaders who you follow already, find three new thought leaders and write down how they will help you grow as a leader. Hint: Googling "Thought leaders in (your field of work)" is a good way to start.

Name   **How will they help me grow?**

1. ___________________   ______________________________
2. ___________________   ______________________________
3. ___________________   ______________________________

What will you do with the knowledge you learn from this group?

____

What holds you back from becoming a thought leader?

____

Now think about that statement again: what's the story you're telling yourself, and what's the truth? Sometimes we hear saboteurs pop up like "you're not a writer" or "who cares what you think?" Don't let these limiting beliefs hold you back. Every thought leader starts off with just a few followers and the more you write, the better you'll get.

Thought Leadership is an Investment

Building recognized expertise will take a year or more, and it forms a foundation you can continue to build on for years to come. This is not a decision to take lightly.

Your Path to Thought Leadership

Your content needs to create conversation and dialogue in the market on an ongoing basis. Here are eight steps to help you create a strong thought-leadership path:

1. Determine where you see yourself as an authority in your industry.
   - Think about the issues and trends impacting your industry and the industries you work closely with. Think about a time you've said to yourself, "But nobody is addressing the problem of ______." or, "I wish someone would talk about ______."
2. Decide who your target audience is.
   - Determine if you want to to external to expand to a bigger audience or internal to support your growth in a specific way.
3. Research your topic.
   - Learn about your audience's priorities, opportunities, and challenges.
4. Follow other thought leaders.
   - Find the subject matter experts on things you like—maybe they're experts on Crossfit, fashion, technology, or they're sales gurus that you watch on LinkedIn. Watch what they do and see where they engage people the most.
5. Build a repository of valuable information that can be easily accessed.
   - Check out Hootsuite or Evernote for ways of distributing and collecting your ideas.
6. Decide on your content strategy: Create, curate, or both.
   - Creating takes a longer commitment; usually about a 500-word article is enough here. You'll need to determine how frequently you want to post, depending on the level of visibility you desire.
   - Curating is sharing others' work, and is a nice, easy way to start the process of adding value but it doesn't take up a ton of time. A blend of both is a great way to provide the most value and strengthens your position as a thought leader.

7. Create consistency.
   - True thought leaders understand that sharing is caring. Schedule time in your calendar for thought leadership.
8. Share your thoughts in a bigger way.
   - Participate in panel discussions at major industry events and seminars attended by target clients and influencers.

Other Tips:

- Talk about current events and movies; be relatable.

- Develop each piece into multiple formats, including videos, infographics, and posts.

- Use shortcuts to help you come up with ideas, like this topic generator for blogs: https://www.hubspot.com/blog-topic-generator.

Putting Theory into Practice: Creating a Strong Thought Leadership Brand

Figure 1.0 My Thought Leadership Brand Architecture

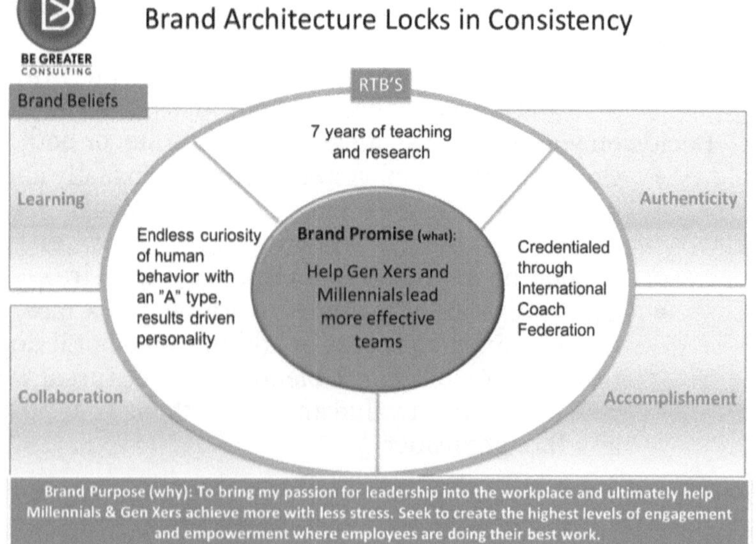

Creating Your Thought Leadership Platform Exercise:

You have been asked to develop a campaign to establish yourself as a thought leader and become one of the leading voices within your industry. Use the image above to create your own thought leadership brand architecture.

If you were to become the industry-leading subject-matter expert, what would you be most passionate about?

Finish this sentence: I'd like to provide thought leadership on ______with a focus on _________.

Thought Leader Topic:

Let's say you're a dentist that is really good at finding shortcuts to back-end office tasks like billing, patient management, and scheduling—the kinds of tasks that dentists have to do but don't enjoy doing as much as dentistry. This thought leader's topic could be something like "I'd like to provide thought leadership on <u>how to get more work done in less time</u> with a focus on <u>dentists</u>." So you'd be helping dentists come up with new and effective ways to save time so they can meet more clients and grow their business.

Brand Purpose is your WHY

Then come up with your purpose, your purpose answers the deeper question of why are you doing the work that you're doing? Here's an example of the "why" for a dentist:

"The joy of changing a person's life by giving him or her a beautiful smile cannot be measured. The satisfaction of restoring a person's dentition so he or she can enjoy food again is worth more than gold. And the opportunity to relieve pain and suffering is a rare privilege."

During your day as a dentist, you do good for a lot of people. You relieve pain and make it possible for people to eat comfortably and enjoy the process. You make it possible for people who haven't smiled in a long time to lay a big, healthy grin on the world and be seen as they really are. You change lives in many, many ways—most of which you will never know. But, occasionally, you will get a heartfelt "thank you" that makes you glow all day. And, once in a while, you may even get a hug and a teary eye that lets you know you are earning your place on this planet. For that, you can take honest satisfaction. The glory, the satisfaction, the joy is in the doing—in knowing that you gave it our best shot; that it may not be "perfect," but that it was as excellent as you were capable of doing at that moment under those circumstances. And with each patient, each time you see them and do something for them, you get still another chance to 'go for the gold.'"

The next step is to take the bigger why and boil it down to a sentence or two. Your purpose isn't shared, it's more for you to get a sense of your "why" for continued inspiration in the work that you do. This dentist's purpose could be:

- To make a positive difference in our patient's health and well being.

The Brand Promise is the WHAT

Then think about what you'll promise with your thought leadership. This is the "what." Following the same example, this dental thought leader is making a promise to:

- Make life for dentists more efficient.

Reasons to Believe (RTBs) is the HOW

RTBs help you explain the proof of how you will fulfill your brand promise. In this case, specifically answering the question "Why should I believe that you specifically are qualified to make life for dentists more efficient?"

Keep it to three if possible, and no more than four reasons you're qualified to take on this topic. RTBs for this dental thought leader could be:
- Proven strategy to cut down back office work time by 50 percent
- Certification in project and time management (provides insights on best practices)
- A lifetime focus on maximizing efficiency and aligning priorities

Your Brand Beliefs are Your Values

Going back to the graphic above, think of these as the cornerstones of what you're all about. A cornerstone is the largest, most solid, and most carefully constructed of any in the edifice. To maintain a strong foundation, everything else depends on these cornerstones.

Our cornerstone is what we're based on—it's the backbone of who we are. It's about the heart of it all. It's our essence. For example:

- Integrity
- Excellence
- Innovation
- Community

These will be the values you selected from Chapter 2. When you write about these areas, you will have that highly charged battery and lots of energy around these topics, so they should be easy to write about.

Completing this brand wheel will serve as your one-pager, allowing your messaging to stay authentic to you and help you stay consistent for your target audience.

Summary

It is your job to prove to everyone else that you're ready for the next step in responsibility to get you closer to getting promoted. It is really up to you to own your career development.

Understanding and applying the four principles of:
- Managing yourself (personal leadership)
- Managing your relationships (servant leadership)
- Managing your manager (followership), and
- Managing your visibility (thought leadership)

will serve as your foundation to transcend whatever differences you may encounter.

It is the equivalent of the lead guitarist having four guitars with him onstage when he performs—one for every genre, every key, and every style of music, using each at just the right time, and with just the right sound! That's music to my ears!

Section IV:

Developing Your Fan Base

11
The Voice Within

Leading Without Authority

Leveraging Mini-Moments to Build Your Leadership

In the last section we looked at four ways to differentiate yourself as a leader and create and sustain a strong leadership brand. So now that you have built up your own leadership competencies, built relationships with your colleagues and boss, and expanded your visibility through thought leadership, it's time to take those fundamental relationship-building components and get real about the day-to-day mini-moments that can make-or-break your leadership soundtrack.

This chapter is about the thing we often complain of not having enough of, and then complain about its pressures when we have it: authority. More specifically, it's about how to lead when you don't have authority.

What if I proposed to you that you could lead more effectively *without* authority than you can with authority?

Stay with me on this, and let's begin this discussion with yet another timeless and universal truth:

Leading is not just for those who manage others. Successful business professionals, regardless of their position, exert influence and are able to lead with or without authority. Directing others requires formal authority. . . leading others requires none.

If you haven't already, at some point in your career you will be given an assignment where you will be responsible for the results but will have no formal authority over the team members who are expected to support you. As we have discussed in previous chapters, these are situations where your "power" or ability to lead will come from your personal leadership rather than any organizational authority bestowed upon you.

Given the fluid roles and responsibilities in today's organizational models, "leading without authority" is occurring more and more. "Don't worry about the organizational chart," your manager tells you. "Just get together with the team and get it done!"

In traditional organizational structures of the past, the question was "Which department is responsible for this?" In today's organizational model, more tailored to the information economy, the question is now "Who is the best person to get this done?"

So, what do you do when you are called upon to, simply, get it done? Will you be ready?

How to Lead Without Authority

So how do you lead effectively and get resourceful in situations where you don't have authority, and you're running into roadblocks with your people?

There are a few "mini-moments" most commonly faced by emerging leaders that can continually impact your career trajectory. These are the situations you may come across where you are not the top dog in the room, yet you still have an opinion and need to speak in a way to ensure you're heard because, ultimately, you are the one responsible for getting the results.

Mini-Moments	**Moment-Making Solutions**
1. Someone is continually pushing against the project you're leading	1. How to tactfully get things back on track
2. Lack of team engagement	2. How to state what you expect without giving ultimatums
3. Managing high levels of team stress and resistance to change or project management	3. How to re-engage others and achieve alignment
4. You think the project is heading in the wrong direction	4. How to tactfully influence others

Mini-Moment #1: Someone is Continually Pushing Against the Project You're Leading

Ah, the recalcitrant rocker . . . doesn't want to play the same tune, thinks the song should be in a different key, wants his solo to be longer. Wherever there are groups, there are resistors. Someone who thinks things should be done a different way or that they should be in charge. Overcoming those situations and winning over those people is one of the ultimate tests of leadership.

Imagine this scenario: You are not the highest-ranking person in the room but you have been assigned to lead the project. Your boss never comes to the meetings so it's up to you to own the timeline and make sure the project runs smoothly. You have a colleague that likes to hear himself talk. It appears he disagrees with your analysis, and he's constantly challenging you and slowing down the project as a result. You are not his boss, yet you need him to step in line, so to speak, to keep the project moving.

Moment-Making Solution #1: How to Tactfully Get Things Back on Track

There is a formula that effective leaders can use to address the reluctant follower. This one was derived from the principles of how to be assertive, and contains three basic components:

1. **Empathy** – Verbally acknowledge the other party's position, ("I realize . . .")

2. **Conflict** – Express the conflict ("However . . .")

3. **Action** – Express the proposed resolution, ("Therefore, I ask that you . . .")

***

Sabrina, a project leader who is responding to Andrea, one of her less-than-enthusiastic senior team members, uses this formula. After several back-and-forths between the two, Sabrina says:

> *I realize that you have often been asked to serve as the project leader, and it may be surprising, or even a little frustrating to have that switched up for this project, I get it.*
>
> *However, Kati (the group manager) asked me to lead this project.*
>
> *Therefore, my request to you is that we simply focus on the task at hand. And if there are any other concerns, I am more than happy to address each of those one-on-one after the meeting.*

With that, the team, including Andrea, proceeds to get on with the "the task at hand." In less than 30 seconds, Sabrina acknowledged Andrea's feelings, let her know they had a job to do, and focused on getting it done.

***

Ask powerful questions that start with "what." Stay away from the bouncer trigger word "why," as it carries judgement that shuts people down. Ask questions that leverage your coaching skills, such as:

- What's important about "x"?
- What other concerns haven't we discussed?
- What does success look like?

It's up to you as a leader to get things tactfully back on track. This leadership quality is part of one of the high performing leadership traits you learned in the "Managing Yourself" chapter. That's right, authenticity. But the Leadership Circle takes this competency one level deeper to "courageous authenticity."

"Courageous authenticity" is about your ability to take tough stands, bring up the "undiscussables" (risky issues the group avoids discussing), openly deal with relationship problems, and share personal feelings/vulnerabilities about a situation. Courage in the workplace involves authentically and directly dealing with risky issues in one-on-one and group situations.

The most important thing to keep in mind in this type of situation is that the best leaders who are also courageously authentic learn how to say no, yet still allow the other person to keep their dignity while doing so.

Mini-Moment #2: Lack of Team Engagement

What many emerging leaders run into is what I call a "bait-and-switch of enthusiasm." You may find a project starts off great with lots of energy, only to notice a few days later that people aren't pulling their weight. High performing leaders tend to get frustrated with this behavior and take on all the work themselves because it needs to be done. That is not what is expected of us as leaders. The earlier on in our careers we can learn the nuances of influence, the more successful our teams will be.

Keeping the Team Focused—The Line Between Too Nice and Too Strict

There is a lively debate in leadership circles about how to best keep team members focused throughout a project. Is it making sure that the team members all get along? Or, is the ultimate objective to get the job done, whether the team members like each other or not?

Some argue that if individuals are going to work together as a team, it is essential that the team members get along with each other—a concept referred to as *"team harmony."* How effective would my beloved Chicago Cubs be if the players did not mesh as a team?

On the other hand, there are those who believe that team harmony is vastly overrated, and that the real focus should be the team objective, or *"goal harmony."* The ultimate focus is winning the World Series, no matter how well the players get along.

Depending on where you sit on that spectrum of "team harmony" versus "goal harmony," you may run the risk of either being too "nicey-nicey" or being known as a "bulldozer."

Being too nicey-nicey may win you some friends, but if you're only focused on team harmony, and thus have a tendency to avoid conflict, you'll let people miss deadlines, work may be sloppy when it's turned in (so you have to do it over for them), and you're probably not going to get the best results you need from your team because you've essentially become a pushover.

On the other hand, giving an ultimatum might get you the results you want, but you might become known as a bulldozer and chances are no one will ever want to work with you again.

If the team is losing steam, and you're noticing reduced levels of energy around the project you're working on, it will impact your ability to get results. Setting expectations might feel like you're creating a tense situation or that you will become disliked by doing so; however, research shows that a little bit of discomfort and tension is actually a part of achieving goal harmony.

Darko Lovric, a principal at Incandescent, talks about this in his HBR article "Too Much Team Harmony Can Kill Productivity":

> *Productive teams are productive because they are able to thrive under tense and difficult circumstances, making the most of disagreements and conflict, while keeping the foundations of their relationships and dynamics intact. Great leaders are able to build teams that can cope with a moderate amount of conflict and tension and to create the conditions for such conflict and tension to arise.*

So how do you walk the line and balance your leadership approach to make sure you're not a pushover *or* a bulldozer, but known for keeping the team focused on getting the work done and achieving your goals?

Moment-Making Solution #2: How to Set Expectations, Without Giving Ultimatums

The foundation of influencing others without issuing ultimatums begins with goal harmony. Everything else follows from there.

How to Set Expectations

You can overcome a conflict as it relates to the task of your project without suffering the cost of the relationship when you have created a balanced approach to team and goal harmony.

If you're leading a cross-functional project for example, and you have a few team members constantly turning in work late or turning in work that has to be re-done, they're at a low level of engagement. If you haven't set any expectations, you've inadvertently set the stage for poor performance because there are no repercussions if someone slacks or doesn't do their work. Letting this behavior continue puts you on the path to ineffective leadership.

Re-engaging your team back into the work involves setting up a boundary. Brené Brown says this in her theworkofthepeople.com video about setting boundaries:

A boundary is saying "Here's what's ok and here's what's not ok." And we are NOT good at setting boundaries. Because we want people to like us, and we don't want to upset anyone. So the way I look at it is B.I.G.

What. . .
- ***B****oundaries need to be in place for me to stay in my*
- ***I****ntegrity and make the most*
- ***G****enerous assumptions about you?*

Why Generous Assumptions are Important

***

There is a company that has two very different VPs. Jenny in marketing is strict and scary and all about perfection when it comes to reporting the numbers. When colleagues Kira, Sarah, and Mary go into a meeting with Jenny, the strict VP, they are off the charts with cortisol. The stress is insane and everyone is nervous, because no one can make a mistake or they'll risk getting yelled at. It feels as though she is full of distrust about the team, and so she doesn't get the best work out of them as a result.

Francesco, on the other hand, is known to start a meeting by saying, "I'm sure everyone is coming into this meeting with good intentions." Everyone looooves that phrase. It creates a safe space for learning to occur. He'll continue with "And I'm expecting great work from all of you, and for our timelines to be met, so we can deliver results in the most effective way possible. I don't like surprises, so can we all agree that you'll let me know in advance if you aren't able to get something in on time?"

No one wants to disappoint Francesco. The whole team wants to give him their best because he believes in the team. He creates the space for honesty, trust, and transparency between everyone in the room, and his expectations are clear.

***

Moving the Needle on Motivation

If someone misses a deadline, the next steps are to figure out the "what" and continue with candor and compassion:

"I noticed the team has missed a few deadlines. Let's share what's going on."

Most leaders really want to tell the team how frustrated they are and how they can't figure out *why* everyone is slacking all of a sudden. Although that's a completely normal thought process, it won't move the needle on their team's motivation. Co-creating the next steps with the team, asking "what" questions, and setting a boundary is the best way forward.

How to Create Goal Harmony

***

Amy is a boss who, when asked a question, always prefaces the answer with the question *"What does success look like?"* In other words, she always wants to know: "What is it we are trying to accomplish?" It also keeps everyone around her focused on the goal. Everything she does or talks about is in the context of *"What's the goal?"*

***

When looking at goal harmony and dealing with someone who has dropped off in their engagement level, you can use a simple technique. This process is straight-up "coaching 101" here, and it's a really effective approach:

1. State the present: "Here's where we're at now."
2. Look to the future: "What does success look like? If we're performing at a 10, what's happening?"
3. Identify the gap: "What barriers need to be removed for us to get to the level of success we've defined? What's getting in our way? What's one thing we can do to move forward?"
4. Create accountability: "How will we hold each other accountable?"

When you notice a lack of engagement, simply bring it up and get curious about what you might not know yet. Stay away from questions like, "If you have questions, let me know," and closed-ended questions like, "Do you have any questions about what to do next?"

Keep questions open-ended and remember that whether you are on the giving or the receiving end of a task, that simple, clarifying question of "What does success look like?" is always a good way to keep everyone focused on the goal.

Powerful, clarifying questions look like, "What questions can I answer?" or "What else would be helpful here?" From these perspectives, any debates that emerge will no longer be about the intended outcome, but about how to best accomplish the desired outcome, and you will have once again fueled the fire to increase the team's energy around the work again.

Mini-Moment #3: Managing High Levels of Team Stress and Resistance to Change or Project Management

We've all been on projects where we are just dreading doing the work. It's usually because the project was designed in a way that doesn't meet our needs, creates more work with no real positive impact, feels like a waste of time . . . you know the drill.

As a project leader who doesn't manage anyone in the group, it's your job when implementing change or managing a project to recognize when stress occurs and take the first step toward resolving it. Your first step is to get a sense of where the individual is coming from. It goes back to Covey's *The 7 Habits of Highly Successful People*: "Seek first to understand, then to be understood." The question is, where does this person reside in terms of their mindset and their level of buy in?

Ann Betz and Ursula Pottinga, co-founders of BeAbove Leadership—a personal, group, and organizational transformation firm—provide a road map of human effectiveness from which to determine our level of effectiveness as leaders. Is your colleague frustrated by something and therefore dragging their feet on moving forward? Or, are they functioning at a higher level and are willing to engage?

BeAbove's Seven Levels of Personal, Group, and Organizational Effectiveness provides a framework from which to monitor yourself and others and guide your interactions with others accordingly. While six levels are pretty self-explanatory, consider the seventh level, synchronicity, as a place where you can get to, but don't often stay. Synchronicity is when someone sees the positive in everything, even if the situation is highly stressful. It's "Dalai Lama land." You can get there, but most can't stay there.

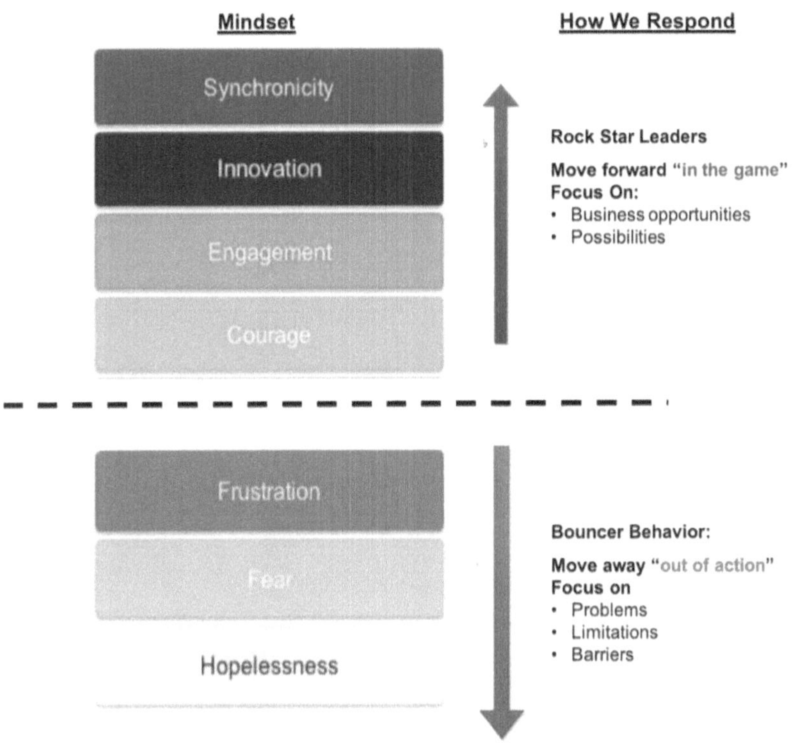

If you are working on a project with others who are "above the line," exhibiting higher levels of leadership such as courage, engagement, or innovation, you have much more willing and engaged team members that will take very little effort to get on board.

However, if a team member has a mindset that's "below the line," for example, someone who is feeling a sense of hopelessness, fear, or frustration, you can assume they are more focused on their internal needs than the task at hand, and that they are in bouncer- resistance mode.

Moment-Making Solution #3: How to Re-engage Others and Achieve Alignment

In those circumstances, it's best to take the following steps:
1. Tune into their frequency—meet them where they're at. This is embodying the "courage" level and it's extremely powerful. If you're engaged with a project and they're not, you're on different frequencies, so they can't hear your music, so to speak. Most people try and push someone up the ladder by telling them that they should be happy because the project is so ahhhmazing!!! Great intention, but, in fact, it often makes the other person feel more alone, less heard, more misunderstood, and more frustrated!
2. Here's how naming the emotion looks when you're tuning in to their level. Think about what *specifically* needs to be acknowledged:
    a. "It sounds like I'm hearing frustration. Am I reading that right?"
    b. "Something feels like it has created frustration. Is that an accurate read?"

    Note: stay with a curious tone on this one and do not use "you." Telling someone "YOU sound frustrated" is a nice way to trigger their bouncer. It implies that the rest of the group is fine while they are the problem child. Keep the comments in neutral, without the "you," for the best results.

3. Leverage active listening and powerful questions about the level they're in. As Daniel Siegel says, you have to "name it, to tame it."
    a. "Tell me about the frustration."
    b. "What else is frustrating?"

    Let them go on until all the stress has been shared. As I always say, stress is like luggage in the brain: once you unpack it, there's more room to think!

So, now that there's more room for rock star level thinking, watch as they move up the ladder to finding solutions, tapping into the "engagement" level, and leveraging "innovation" to find a solution.

It sounds counterintuitive, but the best way to reduce the stress and get people back on board with your project is to shine the light on the stress and talk candidly about what needs to be done to move forward.

Mini-Moment #4: You Think the Project is Heading in the Wrong Direction

I once was on a project where I didn't have as much experience as the project lead, but I *knew* it was heading in the wrong direction. It was one of the most frustrating positions I'd ever been in, as the leader was very confident and very *not* interested in hearing from people with less experience. He also wasn't self-aware of what a disaster the project would be if it kept heading in the direction he was going.

Moment-Making Solution #4: How to Tactfully Influence Others

If this happens to you:

1. Put yourself in your boss's shoes. What might they be seeing that you're not?
2. Get a pulse on the rest of the group. Who else is seeing the same thing but not saying anything? This will help you determine how close or far away you are aligned with the group as a whole with your perspective.
3. Engage the influencers that have the leader's ear and are more open to embracing diversity of thought. See what they think of your concerns.
4. Set up your position in the most strategic way possible. If you can focus on business results, data, or long-term impact it will have more resonance with the senior leader. Ask powerful questions like "Have we ever considered x?" and "What haven't we thought of yet as it relates to this project?"

In his article "How to Disagree with Your Boss," Joseph Grenny, bestselling author of Crucial Conversations and cofounder of VitalSmarts, a leadership training firm, states that there are usually a handful of people who know how to speak truth to power.

They studied the tactics of this group and found that there are ways to disagree effectively. Here are four of the things the study found these people do well:

1. **Contract for candor upfront.** Effective communicators don't wait for the need to disagree—they hold a separate conversation when the stakes are low and emotions are calm to agree with the boss about how to manage those moments when they disagree. This psychological contract becomes a powerful reference point when emotions run high. After all, a boss is much less likely to take offense at disagreement if he or she has invited it in the first place.

2. **Discuss intent before content.** When someone we work with gets defensive, they may believe your dissent is a threat to their goals. Defenses are far less often provoked by actual content than they are by perceived intent. You can be far more candid about your view if you frame it in the context of a mutual purpose that the boss already cares about. If you fail to do this, the boss may believe your disagreement signals a lack of commitment to her interests.

3. **Show respect before dissent.** Most of us assume that if you want to be respectful, you have to dilute your disagreement, and if you want to be honest, you're going to have to hurt some feelings. But this is a false dichotomy. You must find a way to assure your boss that you respect her and her position. When that sense of respect is secure, you can venture into expressing your views openly and honestly.

4. **Ask for—and earn—permission to disagree.** Asking for permission is a powerful way of honoring the position of the boss and avoiding unnecessary provocation. The trick is to ask for permission while giving the boss a reason to give it to you!

Grenny also states that another common way skillful people ensure that dissent is not misinterpreted is by *contrasting*. A *contrast* is a simple "don't mean/do mean" that prevents the boss from misinterpreting your intent. For example, one manager who wanted to express ethical reservations about a boss's decision began, "I'd like to share a concern, but am worried that it will sound like I doubt your character. I don't. And yet I don't think I'd be fully loyal if I didn't share my perspective. May I do so?"

Find a style that's right for you, but stay true to creating a connection. Keep the coaching competencies of powerful questions and active listening in full effect so that the leader can hear you, and so that you're speaking rock star to rock star. You don't want to inadvertently trigger their bouncer who will inevitably block you from getting results. You have ideas, they're worth sharing, and by opening up the conversation, these tactics will help you explore your own perspective and learn something about the leader's point of view as well.

Summary

As you add the concepts of leading without authority, you are developing the ability to sing the song without the lyrics in front of you, and play without sheet music.

That is the point when true rock stars are able to give their full attention to the audience as opposed to a music stand that separates them from their audience.

For chapter resources on how to disagree with your boss and win, visit the resource center at www.begreaterconsulting.com/book (password: rockon).

12

This is How We Do It

Activating Your Success Network

Okay all you budding rock stars, in case you haven't noticed, our approach to building your rock star status has been to work from the "inside out."

We began where all good leadership begins: inside the brain. We examined how to bypass the bouncer with tips and tricks that allow the rock star within you to emerge more often.

We then added the formula for connecting your work to purpose, thus making your job more meaningful.

Next, you were able to fine-tune your four "instruments" as a means to lead and influence others and to have others embrace you, even when you are leading without authority.

Layer by layer, you have established a foundation from which you will stand out from the crowd and distinguish yourself from your peers.

It's now time to look at the long game of leadership. In this chapter we will slowly and methodically build the infrastructure for what, in essence, will be your own personal enterprise, with you acting as president and CEO. No different from Elon Musk, Arianna Huffington, Jack Ma, Donna Karan, or any other influential leader, your network serves as another resource to grow your leadership and your visibility.

Ready to continue?

Activate Your "Success Network": The What, Why, When, Who, & How of It All

What is a "Success Network"?

One of the timeless and universal truths of leadership is that, among other key characteristics, *your effectiveness as a leader is only as good as your network*. The coaches, the thought leaders, and industry experts you deem to be instrumental to your success all make up your "Success Network."

Why Should I Bother?

There are times when you will need guidance. There are times when you will need expert advice. There will be times when you'll hit a rough patch and will need support to help you out of a jam. There will even be times when you'll be up for that promotion and you'll need a good word on your behalf. Like every corporate CEO, as the CEO of "You" Inc., you'll need your own Board of Directors and your own Board of Advisors. Not every day is going to be amazing, and on those not-so-great days, think of your Success Network as a safety net, that, if needed, is there to protect your sanity!

When Should I Start Building a Success Network?

There is never a bad time to start building your network. If you can, do it from the first day you start working. You should also re-evaluate your needs when you get promoted or start working for a new company. In essence, building your Success Network should start from this point forward, if it hasn't already.

Who Should I Include?

You might have informally started building your Success Network externally or inside your own company without even realizing it. Let's take a look. Not including family members, who are your current advisors?

- *Who are the influential or thoughtful individuals you can rally to your cause when needed?*
  1.___________   2.___________   3.___________

- *Who are the people that genuinely listen when you have something to say?*
  1.___________   2.___________   3.___________

- *Who are the people that are eager to sign up when they know you are leading the project?*
  1.___________   2.___________   3.___________

- *Who are the people that are actively supportive and promote your career?*
  1.___________   2.___________   3.___________

If you do not know the answer to those questions, or if you are not impressed with the answers to those questions, or if you are new to the organization and have not had a chance to cultivate a network of advisors, this is where we start.

One example of internal networking is showcased by Limeade, an employee-engagement company in Bellevue, Washington. They encourage employees to start "affinity groups" based on common interests such as golf or cycling, says chief executive Henry Albrecht.

He believes employees who initiate such groups tend to be among those with the highest potential.

So, specifically, if you don't already have a list of people, who should you look for to build your Success Network?

From an internal perspective, think about the people you know that have done really well in the company or have a specific area of expertise that you'd like to learn more about.

You can execute your approach to servant leadership and build your network in a purposeful way at the same time. Even if you're not working with someone on a consistent basis, it doesn't hurt to see if there's anything they need from you and how you might be able to help them. Do that once a quarter to check in with your network as a way to keep your "brand" top of mind.

And the best approach to developing your Success Network is a diverse one, with people from different industries, backgrounds, age groups, ethnic groups, etc. that fit into the roles listed above. The diversity keeps you from getting into "group-think." You want your Success Network to be an outside perspective that not only builds your knowledge as a leader, but expands your thinking in ways you haven't thought of as well.

How Do I Build a Success Network?

You now know the types of individuals to reach out to, but *how* do you go about cultivating your Success Network? Itzik Amiel, bestselling author and international speaker, wrote a book on this very subject, entitled *The Attention Switch: Learn to Switch From Getting Attention to Giving Attention,* and offered these seven ideas on how to cultivate your network.

1. **Never eat alone**: Lunch is a great opportunity to try your internal networking skills. This short time can be very valuable in building strong relationships with your colleagues. Learn what they are busy with, add value to them, and try to help solve their needs.

2. **Participate in internal and external trainings and events:** Try to participate in any training programs and events that the company or your firm offers. Those events are an excellent forum to network and gain new friends and followers.

3. **Become a project leader**: Volunteer to take an assignment or a project. Those are golden opportunities to help the organization, and help you build your network within your company.

4. **Be a supporter to others**: Some of your colleagues have other activities outside of the office, e.g., volunteering in a non-profit organization, helping special institutes etc. You should try to find it out and support your colleague's good causes by attending, volunteering, or donating to their non-profit causes or organizations.

5. **Be a connector or network "broker"**: An easy and rewarding way to practice networking internally is to act as an internal connector. Introduce colleagues when they need a trusted referral in business or life situations such as a dentist, doctor, or plumber.

6. **Be the first to share in moments of joy and sadness:** Be the first to celebrate your colleague's moments of joy; and, likewise, their moments of sadness—from promotion, to the birth of a child, or tragedy.

7. **Brag on your colleagues**: Most people talk naturally about their own achievements. In contrast, praise other colleagues' achievements . . . and really mean it. Bragging on others earns you a supporter for a lifetime.

For more information on *The Attention Switch*, visit www.attentionswitch.com, and visit www.itzikamiel.com for additional resources and programs on networking.

You will be surprised at how much a little goes a long way. And through your career, these people will remember your servant-like approach to all relationships, and in turn, will be ready to help you when needed. In each of these scenarios, it's all about the way we roll as rock stars—shining the spotlight on others, not on ourselves.

How to Build Mutually Beneficial Career-Building Relationships

Rebecca Leder, marketing professional and founder of the relationship building methodology, *The Knock Method: 8 Steps to Building Thriving Career Relationships,* has networked her way to the top. Let's look at how she leveraged networking to propel her career.

She started her own marketing consultancy for small businesses, non-profits, and startups at age 26, and pivoted that experience to advise global media and financial companies at one of the top technology companies in the market.

How does one take such a transformative leap to pivot their career from a small consultancy to the enterprise level? First, marketing was a transferable skill, so she took what she knew and tailored her skills to corporate-level business goals. She says it was about building relationships with individuals with similar roles at select companies she pursued. Second, the hiring manager in an interview helped her see her small business experience as an asset. He said, "If you've been able to convince a business owner with shallow pockets to invest in your services, then certainly enterprises with deeper pockets would also benefit from your skills." A good reminder that it is possible to turn your self-doubts into assets. We are what we listen to.

Prepare to Connect Effectively with Others

It's all about preparation. Leder put extensive energy into researching the people who would be interviewing her and the ins-and-outs of the company—from reviewing their press/media mentions, to following their social media feeds and their stock trends, signing up for product demos, meeting people on the teams she was pursuing, and learning about the leadership team. (Oh, and it's surprising how many people don't sift through a company's website before an interview!) After delving into the ins-and-outs of the company, its culture, hiring needs, and talking to people employed there, she was much more informed to convey how her experience was transferrable to the values of the company she was pursuing a career with, as well as where the gaps were that training or learning-on-the-job time could fill.

Research. It's the first step in preparing to connect with someone worth *pursuing a relationship with*—not pursuing a quick answer, a simple solution, or a one-sided recommendation- rearing request.

Tip: On your way to meet someone for coffee, a meeting, or an informational interview, think through some topics you can discuss in advance, or recall (or search your email/text history) for some personal specifics they shared at the last meeting that you can follow up on to show you were listening. This is a long-term relationship, not a one-time exchange. Prepare to connect.

"If I'm reaching out to someone to partner with, learn from, or pursue a career opportunity with, I already *know* that there's value we can provide each other," says Leder. How? She says it's all about the research and preparation using, for example, publicly available tools and technologies like social media, online portfolios, and "About Us" sections of company websites. Unless the person you're pursuing a connection with is very discreet in the digital world, you're likely to learn something about them that can help you find the best ways to truly connect. Did they go to the same university as you? Are they from the same hometown? Do they volunteer time for similar causes to those you value? Find that commonality and bring it forward in your communications so you can connect on a human level. If all else fails, ask a mutual contact for background information so you can tailor your message.

Does Investing So Much Time and Energy on an Individual Person and Company Level Work?

Yes! In fact, to further prove her eight-step relationship building method works, Rebecca has not only connected with, but has also interviewed a variety of successful professionals. Her networking contacts range from a Wharton professor, to a founder of a school, to a film producer, and an apparel brand founder all in order to learn about how they have built relationships and secured help along their journey.

She's received a reply from each person she has set out to interview, so she has proof that the method works, and she has a powerful network of solid relationships as a result of her sharing their success stories.

Don't be afraid to "go big or go home!"

When reaching out to one such CEO, whom she follows on Instagram and Linkedin, she timed her email to when she noticed the CEO was back home after being out of the country. This helped her not only personalize her message based on publicly shared info, it also helped maximize the chances she'd get a reply and provided an opportunity to include a personal topic of conversation by being able to ask how the trip went.

Besides research, other steps in the *The Knock Method* include proving you're invested in the relationship, and showing compassion and helping others, thus building a positive reputation.

Next-Level Networking

As you continue building relationships throughout your career, invest in each relationship before it even takes shape. It's about quality, not quantity. Truly get to know those you're preparing to meet with, which will set you up for more fruitful conversations, discovery of new ways to help each other, mutual benefits, and time that's worth everyone's time.

For more information on how to build your network check out www.theknockmethod.com.

One Note for Women

As co-authors Sally Helgesen & Marshall Goldsmith state in their book *How Women Rise: Break the 12 Habits Holding You Back from Your Next Raise, Promotion, or Job,* "The high value women place on relationships often makes them more eager to seek out personal friendships than to cultivate connections and collect chits for future use." Men, on the other hand, tend to be more purposeful and look at what's referred to as "Leveraged Networking." This means pursuing people that help them accomplish their objectives.

The authors continue to share that "Leverage is used to achieve both tactical and strategic goals. You initiate leverage when you make a request. Usually, the request is small and specific. Something like: 'I'm representing an artist whose prints are for hotel lobbies. Do you know anyone in the hotel business who could introduce me to dealers who work for their properties? Would you be willing to share your insights about what motivates this client?'"

These are the tactical favors that help you accomplish immediate objectives—things that would be helpful this week, this month, this year. Yet at its most effective, leverage also serves the larger strategic purpose of engaging those who might be helpful to you in the future. This kind of reciprocity works best when your goals harmonize and complement those of the people you seek to engage.

The authors continue to share that the leveraged network has a specific purpose in mind, which means you use different criteria than when you establish a friendship:

- Does the person you seek to engage have relationships that could be useful to you now or in the future?
- Does she seem poised to become more powerful over time?
- Is there something you're particularly well positioned to offer him now that might make him eager to be a resource for you in the future?

Remember that leveraged networking benefits are measurable and concrete. You gain a new group of potential clients or investors, you have the opportunity to enhance your reputation and visibility or learn a new skill. Look to find leveraged partners who not only can deliver for you, but who you can deliver for as well.

Ladies, one last thing: If this feels icky, I get it. It seems like it's a selfish move, but it's not. You *will* have something to offer them in return, if not now, then in the future.

Women tend to get in an either-or mentality: either you're a good person who only helps others advance or you're a selfish person who uses others to achieve your own agenda. You can be *both* a caring person *and* capable of pursuing your own self-interest. The authors suggest that women simply think about taking their strengths in networking to become more *intentional* in building relationships that may be advantageous to them in the future.

The key is remembering that you will add value to their cause as well.

As a final perspective, a famous rock star once shared her thoughts on the power of a having a network, as well. She was once lauded by a music critic for putting on a dazzling concert performance, and when asked about her success, she simply said, "Just look at the group I have supporting me. They are the key to any success I enjoy."

Like a rock star or any other successful performer or leader, your success is highly dependent on the group supporting you. Choose them wisely, nurture them well, and acknowledge them often.

Summary

Having a diverse network of advisors and influencers is like having your own backup band to accompany you. Being able to lead without authority is like being able to play without the music in front of you.

So, hit the stage rock stars. You are ready to rock!

Conclusion

Started From the Bottom Now We Here

OK, Rockers . . . there you have it!

Welcome to the club of rock stars. As you come in, go to the front of the line, past the bouncer, and take a look around. What do you see?

You see people being thoughtful and engaging when they talk about goals, objectives, purpose, and tactics. You see people discussing company and personal values. You see people not telling their own thoughts, but asking others about *their* thoughts. You see them genuinely listening to each other.

Even when there are differences, you see the differing parties pausing, taking a breath and deliberately responding, not from a position of right or wrong, but from a position of active listening and exploring the issue further to better understand why someone may have a different point of view. You see them learning from each other and gaining a more enlightened viewpoint.

What do you *not* see?

You *don't* see individuals flipping their lids, trying to exert their leadership to prove that they're the smartest person in the room. You don't see them trying to prove anything. You *don't* hear debates about who is right and who is wrong. Even when being confronted with their own mistakes or shortcomings, you don't hear them retaliate or attempt to defend themselves. Rather than dispute feedback, you see them attempting to learn from it. They are very comfortable with themselves and their work. Their discussions are grounded in a sense of purpose and values that are aligned to the work they do. They are not there to compete with anyone.

In fact, rather than compete, they look for ways to enhance the success of their colleagues and leaders. Being comfortable with themselves, they are equally comfortable being followers, looking for ways to make their leaders successful. Even in leadership positions, their focus is not how they can be successful, but how they can help others be successful. They do not boast of their own accomplishments but of the accomplishments of others.

There is a level of humility about them that could cause one to wonder if they have the toughness to lead. That is, until you see how they challenge poor performance. And even then, there is an element of humility in the way they do it. They maintain their respect for the individual, while challenging the individual's performance, helping them optimize their potential.

In the introduction of this book we spoke of the many paradoxes of leadership. We spoke of how "rock stars" are accustomed to having the spotlight directed at them, and, therefore, to lead and inspire, one must demand that same spotlight. Yet, the reality is those who are able to lead or inspire others tend to shift the spotlight away from themselves, shine it on others, and ask, "How can I help you?" Through this approach, we explained, successful leaders find that by helping others, their own success, money, and rock star status have naturally followed. They don't chase the spotlight. The spotlight finds them.

Through this book, we said we wanted you to learn how next-generation leaders differentiate themselves, stand out, and succeed in today's workplace.

My goal was to pack all the content from a leadership coaching engagement into a package of battle-tested, next-generation leadership lessons in one playbook.

Just like major leaguers or NFL superstars, the need for coaching never ends. The need for accountability, reinforcement, and continuous improvement is an ongoing process. As Snoop Dogg says, "Surround yourself with people who are better than you, so you can get better."

You always have room to "Be Greater." So, this playbook, much like how it functions in sports, does not replace the need for coaching. And whether you're starting off in one of your first jobs, or are a few years into a career and looking to make that leap to the next level, you now have the framework from which to rise up, stand out, and lead like a rock star.

Welcome to the club, rock stars!

Rock on!

RISE UP

Bibliography

INTRODUCTION

STILL FACE EXPERIMENT: Tronick, E., Als, H., Adamson, L., Wise, S., and Brazelton, T. B. "Infants' Response to Entrapment Between Contradictory Messages in Face-to-Face Interaction." *Journal of the American Academy of Child and Adolescent Psychiatry*, no. 17 (1978): 1–13. Retrieved on on 2019 ,January 11 from https://www.youtube.com/watch?v=apzXGEbZhto

MILLENNIAL AND GEN-Z PERCENT OF WORKFORCE STATISTIC: retrieved on 2019, January 11 from https://www.politifact.com/virginia/statements/2015/jun/15/mark-warner/warner-says-millennials-will-have-75-percent-jobs-/.

NUMBER OF MILLENNIALS IN THE WORKFORCE: Fry, R. (2018, April 11). "Millennials Are Largest Generation in the U.S. Labor Force." Retrieved on 2019 ,January 11 from http://www.pewresearch.org/fact-tank/2018/04/11/millennials-largest-generation-us-labor-force/.

DEFINING THE GENERATIONS: Dimock, M. (2018, March 01). "Where Millennials End and Post-Millennials Begin." Retrieved from http://www.pewresearch.org/fact-tank/2018/03/01/defining-generations-where-millennials-end-and-post-millennials-begin/.

CHATPER 1

ORIGIN OF AMYGDALA: "Awesome Information About the Location and Functions of the Amygdala." (2018, May). Retrieved from https://bodytomy.com/amygdala-function.

THE AMYGDALA: Goleman, D. *Emotional intelligence*. London: Bloomsbury, 2004.

CORTISOL AND CHRONIC STRESS: Millard, E. (March 2016). "The Cortisol Curve." Retrieved from https://experiencelife.com/article/the-cortisol-curve/

DRUNK MONKEYS: Gallagher, B. (2011). "Buddha: How To Tame Your Monkey Mind." Retrieved from https://www.huffingtonpost.com/bj-gallagher/buddha-how-to-tame-your-m_b_945793.html

VICTIM STATE: Dyer, Wayne. *Your Erroneous Zones: Step-by-step Advice for Escaping the Trap Of Negative Thinking and Taking Control of Your Life*. New York, NY: HarperPerennial, 1991.

PREFRONTAL CORTEX FUNCTIONS adapted from: Siegel, Daniel J. The Mindful Brain: Reflection and Attunement in the Cultivation of Well-Being. W.W. Norton, 2007.

80% OF LEADERS ARE REACTIVE: Anderson, R., & Adams, W. (2018). Reactive Leadership - The Leadership Circle. Retrieved from https://leadershipcircle.com/reactive-leadership/ Excerpted from Anderson, R., & Adams, W. (2015). Mastering leadership: An integrated framework for breakthrough performance and extraordinary business results. Hoboken, NJ: Wiley.

BENEFITS OF MEDITATION: Davis, D. M. (n.d.). What are the benefits of mindfulness. Retrieved on 2019, January 11 from https://www.apa.org/monitor/2012/07-08/ce-corner.aspx

BENEFITS OF MEDITATION Davis, D. M., & Hayes, J. A. (2011). What are the benefits of mindfulness? A practice review of psychotherapy-related research. *Psychotherapy, 48*(2), 198-208. doi:10.1037/a0022062

TRANSCENDENTAL MEDITATION: How does TM work? Retrieved on 2019, January 11 from https://www.tm.org/transcendental-meditation Transcendental Meditation Technique - A Complete Introduction. Retrieved from https://youtu.be/fO3AnD2QbIg

CHAPTER 2

FUNCTIONS OF THE PFC: Prefrontal Cortex. Retrieved on 2019, January 11 from https://en.wikipedia.org/wiki/Prefrontal_cortex

LIFE PURPOSE: Kimsey-House, H., Kimsey-House, K., Sandahl, P., & Whitworth, L. (3rd ed)
 (2011). Co-active coaching: Changing business, transforming lives. London: Nicholas Brealey Publishing.

CHAPTER 3

GALLUP STATISTIC: Harter, J. Employee Engagement on the Rise in the U.S. Gallup, Inc. 2018, August 26 Retrieved from https://news.gallup.com/poll/241649/employee-engagement-rise.aspx

STRENGTHS: CliftonStrengths Solutions for Individuals accessed on 2019, January 11 from https://www.gallupstrengthscenter.com/ formerly Clifton StrengthsFinder at time of coaching (2018).

YOU DON'T NEED AN MBA TO BE HAPPY: The Parable of the Mexican Fisherman: Anonymous

GOING BACKWARDS TO GO FORWARD: 65 Back. *Content courtesy of Ram S. Ramanthan, MCC*
2017, June 12 https://coachfederation.org/blog/build-your-business-with-your-heart ® Coacharya. All Rights Reserved.

ECKART TOLLE: Tolle, E., & DiCarlo, R. E. (2016). *The power of now: A guide to spiritual enlightenment.* London: Yellow Kite.

CHAPTER 4

FEEL THE FEAR: Jeffers, S. J. (2007). *Feel the fear and do it anyway: How to turn your fear and indecision into confidence and action.* London: Vermilion.

CHAPTER 5

BOUNDARIES AND BIG: *Brené Brown on Setting Boundaries-* Segment with Brené Brown on empathy, compassion and boundaries, The Work of the People Films, retrieved on 2019, January 10 from
https://www.youtube.com/watch?v=BESvQB6J5rc

FLIPPING YOUR LID: Siegel, D. J. (2011). *Mindsight: The new science of personal transformation.* New York: Bantam Books.

OPRAH COMMENCEMENT SPEECH: *Oprah Winfrey Gives Commencement Speech at USC.* Retrieved on 2019, January 10 from https://www.c-span.org/video/?443945-1/oprah-winfrey-commencement-speech-usc

HOW STRESS IMPACTS THE BODY: The Effects of Stress on Your Body. Retrieved on 2019, January 10 from
https://www.healthline.com/health/stress/effects-on-body#1

CHAPTER 6

NEUROPLASTICITY: Medeiros, J. (2017, October 04). "How to 'Game Your Brain': The Benefits of Neuroplasticity." Retrieved from https://www.wired.co.uk/article/game-your-brain.

TM: El-Sheikh, T. (2018, October 26). Scicasts.com is now part of Mindzilla's Knowledge Portal. Retrieved from
https://scicasts.com/channels/neuroscience/2065-cognitive-science/13464-new-study-highlights-unique-state-of-restful-alertness-during-transcendental-meditation/

TM: *Publication: **fMRI during Transcendental Meditation practice.**Michelle C.Mahone et al. Brain and Cognition (2018):*

MEDITATION: Retrieved on January 10, 2019 from
https://www.webmd.com/pain-management/news/20060809/meditation-may-help-brain-handle-pain

STRESS: Retrieved on January 10, 2019 http://blog.ch.tm.org/uncategorized/5-new-findings-about-stress-and-how-tm-can-help/

MEDIATION AND SLEEP: Retrieved on January 10, 2019 http://www.mindmojo.co/journal/2017/7/24/meditation-vs-sleep

MEDITATION & ATTENTION Retrieved on January 10, 2019 https://en.wikipedia.org/wiki/Gamma_wave, https://news.wisc.edu/brain-scans-show-meditation-changes-minds-increases-attention/

DEEPER LEVELS OF SLEEP: Retrieved on January 10, 2019 https://eocinstitute.org/meditation/require-less-sleep-with-meditation-460/#codeword2

REWIRING: Retrieved on January 10, 2019 http://reset.me/story/neuroplasticity-the-10-fundamentals-of-rewiring-your-brain/
INSPIRATION Retrieved on January 10, 2019 https://hbr.org/2017/04/how-to-be-an-inspiring-leader
IMPACT Retrieved on January 10, 2019   http://www.development.org.nz/news-and-views/how-to-have-impactful-crucial-conversations/

Neuroplasticity: Retrieved on January 10, 2019 https://www.medicinenet.com/script/main/art.asp?articlekey=40362)

CHAPTER 7

ALL LEADERSHIP COMPETENCY AND ASSESSMENT MATERIAL REFERENCED: Courtesy of The Leadership Circle®, all rights reserved.

ADDITIONAL READING REFERENCED ON SELF-DISCOVERY:
Goldsmith, M., & Reiter, M. (2007). *What got you here won't get you there: How successful people become even more successful.* New York: Hyperion.

CHAPTER 8
SERVANT LEADERSHIP: Greenleaf, R., Retrieved on Jan 10, 2019 from https://www.greenleaf.org/what-is-servant-leadership/

CHAPTER 9

What does it mean to MANAGE UP: Reynolds, J. What Does It Mean to Manage Up? Retrieved on 2019, January 10 from Tiny Pulse https://www.tinypulse.com/blog/what-does-it-mean-to-manage-up

GALLUP REPORT: *How Millennials Want to Work and Live, The Six Big Changes Leaders Have to Make.* Gallup, Inc. © 2016 All Rights Reserved

BE BOLD WITH YOUR BOSSES: Chaleff, I. (2009). *The courageous follower: Standing up to & for our leaders.* San Francisco: Berrett-Koehler.

QUALITIES ESSENTIAL TO GOOD FOLLOWERSHIP: HURWITZ, M. (2017). *LEADERSHIP IS HALF THE STORY: A fresh look at followership, leadership, and collaboration.* Toronto. Rotman-UTP Publishing.

CHAPTER 10

THOUGHT LEADERSHIP ORIGIN: The term, although also stated to have originally been sourced by The Thestic Annual in 1875 describing Ralph Waldo Emerson: M, P. C. (Ed.). (1875). *The Thestic Annual for 1875.* Calcutta: Calcutta Central Press Company, 1875.
 in its modern popular usage was first coined in 1994 by Joel Kurtzman, the Founding Editor of Strategy+Business magazine (published by the American management consulting company Booz & Company) for the "Thought Leaders" series of one-to-one interviews with high profile business people, academics, and authors.
Li, Zhan. (2016, December 13). "The History and Future of 'Thought Leadership.'" Retrieved from http://www.globalinfluence.world/en/history-future-thought-leadership/.

THE WHY FOR A DENTIST: Glasscoe, D. (1998, August 01). Why would anyone want to become a dentist? Retrieved from http://www.dentaleconomics.com/articles/print/volume-88/issue-8/features/why-would-anyone-want-to-become-a-dentist.html

THOUGHT LEADERS ARE CREATORS: DREZNER, D. W. (2019). The Ideas Industry: How Pessimists, Partisans, and Plutocrats are Transforming the Marketplace of Ideas. Oxford. OXFORD UNIV Press.

WHAT MAKES A STRONG THOUGHT LEADER: KNILANS, G. (2016, January 05). Thought Leadership: What it is and Why it is Important. Retrieved from https://richtopia.com/effective-leadership/thought-leadership-important

CHAPTER 11

COURAGEOUS AUTHENTICITY: Interpreting your LCP Brochure, **The Leadership Circle®, all rights reserved.** The Leadership Circle retrieved from https://www.fcg-global.com/s/Interpreting-Your-LCP.pdf
Longer version:
https://intra.trustmarkins.com/intranet/leadershipsummit2016/pdfs/CA_Webinar.pdf

EMBRACE CONFLICT IN TEAMS: Lovric, D., & Chamorro-Premuzic, T. (2018). *Too Much Team Harmony Can Kill Creativity.* Retrieved from https://hbr.org/2018/06/too-much-team-harmony-can-kill-creativity. Harvard Business Review.

Setting Boundaries: The Work of the People presents Brene Brown: Setting Boundaries. Retrieved on 2019, January 11 from https://www.theworkofthepeople.com/boundaries

SEEK FIRST TO UNDERSTAND: Covey, S. R. (2014). *The 7 habits of highly effective people: Powerful lessons in personal change.* New York: Free Press.

HOW TO DISAGREE WITH YOUR BOSS: Grenny, J. (2014, November 25). *How to Disagree with Your Boss.* Retrieved from https://hbr.org/2014/11/how-to-disagree-with-your-boss. Harvard Business Review.

SEVEN LEVELS: Seven Levels of Personal, Group, and Organizational Effectiveness
Betz, A., and Pottinga, U., Be Above, retrieved on January 10, 2019 from https://www.beaboveleadership.com/

<u>CHATPER 12</u>

CULTIVATING YOUR NETWORK: Amiel, I. (2014). *The Attention Switch.* Filament Publishing.

WOMEN AND NETWORKING: Helgesen, S., & Goldsmith, M. (2018). *How women rise: Break the 12 habits holding you back from your next raise, promotion, or job.* New York: Hachette Books.

REBECCA LEDER www.theknockmethod.com (2019) *The Knock Method: 8 Steps to Building Thriving Career Relationships* © All Rights Reserved.